# PULLING THE PUNCHES

## DEFEATING DOMESTIC VIOLENCE

# ABOUT THE AUTHOR

Luke Daniels is a social activist, counsellor and consultant on domestic violence, who was born in Guyana and settled with his family in London in the 1970s. A father of eight, he believes passionately in the need for men to take an active role in parenting. He was the first co-ordinator of a Black Fathers project and has worked with youths in schools. He has had years of experience working with couples seeking help to overcome difficulties in their relationships. His work counselling men at the Everyman Centre in London received national recognition in the 1992 television documentary "Pulling the Punches".

# PULLING THE PUNCHES
## Defeating Domestic Violence

by
## Luke Daniels

*For All Students of W M C*

*Luke*
*2/11/11*

BOGLE *L'ouverture* PRESS

LONDON

Cover & layout design
by Mervyn Weir

ISBN: 979-904 521 583-8

Bogle-L'Ouverture Press
P.O. Box 2186
Ealing, London W13 9ZQ.

For my children:

Oliver, Jason, Bryce, Fidelle, Kaya, Femi, Bibsi, Zak;
and for those who have adopted me: Aaron, Mbugwah,
Jennah, Malike and Azania.

## ACKNOWLEDGEMENTS

Writing this book would have been much harder without the support and encouragement of some key people in my life.

Acknowledgement is first of all due to my Mom Olga, without whom I would not be here to have produced this book.

Marilyn, my ex-wife, was the catalyst for my work with perpetrators, and - despite threats of lawsuit if the writing was not to her liking - I know is backing me. My close relationship with Sonya has borne the brunt of many absences yet she never failed to push me to get on with it.

Many among my family and friends have given me their unstinting support - too many to mention everyone by name here, but among those to whom I extend particular thanks are:

Tara Raj for reading and making comments; Alex Vincenti for encouragement, belief and seeking out information on the web; Deborah for providing helpful tips and a book on getting published. Cousins Eve and Tivane and Aunt Aloma showed unreserved belief in my ability to produce this book. Jean Martin has been unflinching in her belief that this book will make a significant difference to people's lives; and Isha McKenzie-Mavinga has given loving support and encouragement over many years.

I am grateful to Mmatshilo Motsei for her encouragement and the opportunity to do this work in South Africa, and to Ngao Motsei, who made her beautiful home in Johannesburg available to me for three months to get the project really started. Rod Prince and Judith Amanthis have both given encouragement and practical help along the way. I learned much from many of my clients at the Everyman Centre and from colleagues there with whom I journeyed - Paul Wolflight, Roger Koester and Neil Huggins. Many of my co-counsellors have listened to me over the years. Arthur has read and given me useful feedback as a perpetrator.

Making the move from handwritten to computer text was a huge leap encouraged by my friend and comrade Leland DeCambra, and his continued technical support has been invaluable.

Last but not least, Margaret Busby made a patient and skilful contribution towards bringing the book project to conclusion and is a source of inspiration.

# CONTENTS

# INTRODUCTION

Domestic violence is one of the most pressing social issues affecting societies in the world today. Men of every nation, race, class, religion and age are responsible for the mistreatment of women, through domestic violence. All countries are implicated in this crime. In Britain, partners murder 120 women and 30 men every year.[1] In the USA a woman suffers domestic violence every 15 seconds and four women are killed every day by a partner.[2] In India more than 7,000 women are murdered by their families and in-laws in disputes over dowries each year.[3] In South Africa every six hours a man kills his partner.[4] In Turkey, one in two women suffers domestic violence.[5] The same is true for Zimbabwe.[6] In Russia every 40 minutes a woman is killed by her partner[7] — and the slaughter goes on and on.

With such levels of violence against women it is easy to understand why the still taboo issue of women perpetrators is seen as a diversion in some quarters, despite recent research showing that an "equal number of men and women had been assaulted by a current or former partner" and that "one in four women and one in six men will suffer domestic violence at some stage in their lives". The survey also shows that women are twice as likely to have been injured by a partner.[8] According to Amnesty International, one in three women has been beaten, raped or otherwise abused.[9] Whatever the true figure, hundreds of millions of women and men globally are unable to live happy, fulfilling lives, free from fear, as a result of this mistreatment; a violation of their basic human rights.

This self-help book is for perpetrators, men and women all over the world, who for whatever reasons may never have the opportunity to see a counsellor. It is also for anyone concerned about the use of violence and for those who are afraid that they may use violence in the future. I hope that practitioners in the field of domestic violence will also find something useful here, but the focus is on perpetrators who want to stop their violent behaviour. The book is based on years of experience of working mainly with men and more recently working with women perpetrators. My group-work experience with perpetrators was entirely with men but the issues raised in the groups are relevant to all perpetrators, male or female. I share a lot about myself in the book because I feel it is important that the "client" knows something about the counsellor and his/her world-view and also something about their counselling perspective. I believe that the more perpetrators understand about the process of change and the causes of their violent behaviour the faster they will progress once they make the "decision" to stop their violence. I ask perpetrators to be open and honest with me in their sessions. It is only fair that I do the same with them, hence I share that I too once perpetrated domestic violence.

I have omitted issues of race and class that were part of the original "group-work" sessions I led at the Everyman Centre. Most groups were of mixed race and class and I felt it important for the "openness" and safety in the group that these issues not be ignored. They do not arise in the same way in a self-help book. Race and class are crucial issues in ending all oppression but they may be better addressed in a separate publication.

Each chapter looks at a key "awareness-raising" issue in the struggle to defeat domestic violence. The first chapter explores the Roots of Domestic Violence - it has a beginning and must have an ending. The second chapter, Men's Liberation, looks at how the oppression of men is responsible for much of the violence we face in the world today. Chapter Three is about Women's Liberation; we cannot hope to stop violence to women if sexism is allowed to reign supreme. Some perpetrators hit their partners while under the influence of mind-altering substances, so the fourth chapter is on Giving Up Addictions. There would be no perpetrators if children were not hurt, mistreated, neglected, misinformed and socialized to be violent in the first place, so Chapter Five is on Parenting for Change. The sixth and final chapter is Building Loving Relationships; many perpetrators profess their undying love yet abuse their partners.

It should not surprise that men are the main perpetrators of domestic violence as the establishment of patriarchal society depended on men being prepared to use violence to dominate women. Patriarchy positively encouraged and often coerced men to be violent to women. This and the myth that men are violent by nature have been ongoing for millennia, resulting in many men internalizing the notion and acting it out on each other and on women. This violent stereotyping of masculinity must be challenged and discontinued as part of the strategy for ending male violence to women. By focusing only on male perpetrators, as some advocate, we "reinforce the stereotype of men as violent".[10] Also, by ignoring women's violence we deny women perpetrators the support they need to stop their violent behaviour, leaving many women and male survivors with no hope that the violence will end. We should bear in mind that it is not only heterosexual relationships that are problematic and we should not ignore the 1 in 3 partners in same-sex relationships who suffer domestic violence.[11]

In Britain, where domestic violence accounts for a quarter of all reported crime, a report is made to the police every minute, costing the criminal justice system £1 billion a year. The emotional and financial cost to society is huge, because families are dislocated, or because survivors cannot work as a result of injury, or because perpetrators are imprisoned. The cost to the British economy is £5.8 billion a year. Of this the cost to business was £2.7 billion, the cost to medical and social services some £3.1 billion according to government figures,[12] although the actual cost is likely to be much higher considering that not all domestic violence crimes are reported to the police. Whatever the true figures, the distress and damage caused to children's lives is incalculable; figures in Britain show that, in half the cases of domestic violence, children under 16 years of age were in the household at the time.[13] Other studies show that in 9 out of 10 cases, children are in the same room or one adjacent to where the abuse is happening.[14] I believe the witnessing of domestic violence by children has a detrimental effect on them later in life; the vast majority of male perpetrators I have worked with saw or heard domestic violence in their childhood.

In Japan, where domestic violence was made an offence in 2001, the figures for 2006 show a 17 per cent increase on 2005. This massive increase, campaigners believe, could be a result of victims overcoming the "cultural taboos that once forced them to stay silent".[15] Some of the apparent increase in female perpetrators in Britain could, similarly, be as a result of men now feeling able to report this abuse.

For too long, violence in the home was ignored, seen as "just a domestic" by the police. This encouraged many perpetrators to act with impunity. Now all police forces in Britain have a domestic violence unit, with trained officers capable of responding when called to a domestic violence incident. These improvements are to be welcomed, but there is still too much inconsistency in the way different forces respond to domestic violence, and there have been some spectacular failures involving the loss of life as a result of complacency on the part of the force about protecting women. The response to calls for help all too often depends on the attitude of senior officers and/or the officers on the ground. Some studies show that in some countries the incidence of domestic violence is higher in the police force than in the population at large.[16] This is bound to affect on the way officers respond to domestic violence incidents.

Exposing domestic violence is the first step towards ending it. We owe much to the feminist movement for getting this issue on the agenda and in keeping it there. Suffering domestic violence in silence is not an option as this only encourages the perpetrator, who commonly tries to cover up the abuse by isolating the survivor from family and friends. It is important that survivors expose the abuse and seek help, but research shows that only 60 per cent of survivors do so. Similarly it is imperative that perpetrators get help to stop their violence, but often there is no one for them to turn to.

With less tolerance for domestic violence nowadays, what was legally acceptable behaviour in the past is now no longer permissible in law in most developed countries. After being encouraged by patriarchy for millennia to mistreat women, men are now expected to change their oppressive behaviour almost overnight, with little support for change from the state. Although a clear message must be sent to perpetrators that their violence is wrong and will no longer be tolerated, to only promote "long prison sentences" as the solution to the problem has proved to be counter-productive. Some had long argued that threats of lengthy prison sentences for perpetrators would leave many survivors more vulnerable as some will be more reluctant to call the police, if they think their partner will be put away for a long time. This thinking seems to have been vindicated when the Ministry of Justice confirmed that it was setting up a meeting with Judges to discuss the situation after a new law toughening the penalties for domestic violence seemed to have 'backfired' with fewer survivors of domestic violence seeking non–molestation orders.[17]

Often the response to domestic violence has been to punish the perpetrator, with little or no attempt at changing their behaviour. Although the prison approach may be effective in stopping the violence in some people and may even deter some, it does not bring about the change in attitude necessary for a permanent solution to the problem also some studies suggest that imprisonment can make people more violent.[18] To make a real difference in the fight against domestic violence we need sensible policy and long-term planning that includes work with perpetrators outside the criminal justice system.

In England, with a prison system bursting at its seams and limited resources making rehabilitation a low priority, there are also fundamental problems with working for change in prisons, as highlighted by the experience of one (unnamed) drug counsellor.[19] She wrote:

> *"Prison hardens people or it breaks their heart," to paraphrase Oscar Wilde, and I saw this on a daily basis. Prison workers either became cynical — and dehumanised the prisoners with labelling, emotional coldness and a disgust at their existence - or they became disillusioned and angry. Usually at that point they left.*
>
> *I left for two reasons. First, I had listened for months to horror stories about the brutality of the prison system, the abuse many prisoners had experienced while in children's homes and at the hands of their parents-and about the crimes, many of them terrible to hear of, that brought them to prison. One guy in his early twenties had never known anything but violence and oppression. His life was one long escape into heroin, violent crime and then being caught and brutalized by the prison system. He felt total despair. He could not believe in rehabilitation, he said, because all prisons were run on brutality and violence, not necessarily overtly physical, but always the threat lurking, that you could be taken to the punishment block and beaten and there would be nothing you or anyone else could do.*
>
> *I realised I was colluding in the lie that rehabilitation can take*

*place in an atmosphere of such overwhelming, callousness and threat. I could not do it anymore.*

She is not the only one disaffected with the prison system; one of England's most senior judges, Lord Phillips of Worth Matravers, the Lord Chief Justice, described prisons as "social dustbins" where it is "difficult or impossible" to rehabilitate prisoners. He said it was "madness to spend £37,000 jailing someone when, by spending much less on services in the community, you can do as good a job". He calls for better resources for projects in the community: "it's no answer just to put more and more people in prison," he said.[20]

Although imprisonment must remain an option, and extreme and persistent offenders must be seen to be punished, those who call for long prison sentences for perpetrators should bear in mind that some judges sentence women more severely for committing what are perceived as "male" offences. Imprisonment for women is especially harsh, and women account for almost 20 per cent of suicides in British prisons while making up only 6 per cent of the prison population.[21] Their children also suffer; research shows that "children with a parent in prison are more likely to suffer with mental health problems".[22] The number of women in prison has more than trebled over the last decade and the situation for them and their children seems set to get worse as Britain contemplates building the largest women's jail in Europe. This despite calls for less imprisonment of women by the then Prime Minister's wife.[23]

If all countries adopted a strategy of imprisonment for every perpetrator, the worldwide prison population would soar to unacceptable heights. It is estimated that more than 9.8 million people, mostly men, are in prisons around the world. About half are in the USA (2.29m), China (1.57m) and Russia (0.89m). England has over 80,000 and rising. This imprisonment has an effect on 150.000 children each year in England alone and it is estimated that at any one time 8 per cent or 100,000 children have a father in jail. To add significantly to these numbers would increase the hardship for many more children and would be a burden on the taxpayer.

Most survivors of domestic violence wish only for the violence to end, not for their partners to be imprisoned; indeed, survivors of domestic violence often see the "good side" to the perpetrator. Perpetrators often hate themselves for their violence and are crying out for help. After Pulling the Punches, a documentary on the Everyman Centre's work, was shown on television, there were over 500 calls to the helpline set up on the night.[25] The calls were mostly from men but some women also sought help with their violent behaviour.

Having counselled hundreds of men over a five-year period at the Everyman Centre in London I am very aware of the need for places for perpetrators who want to change. Our waiting-list for men self-referring could be a year long and we were sometimes forced to close the list since we were working with limited resources. There are not enough projects capable of providing face-to-face counselling for even a fraction of the perpetrators who need counselling, and need it urgently. This is what one perpetrator wrote (names and dates have been changed):

*Dear Mr Daniels*

*My name is Barry, I am 24 years old as you can see I am in Brixton Prison, I am waiting to go up for sentence on the 10th June, I have been here for almost 3 months. This is the 3rd time I have come to prison for being violent towards my girlfriend Sharon, we have a baby girl Jane and she is 4 years old and we have a baby boy who is six years old, whose name is John, he is from a relationship Sharon had before me, for about 3 years. I have always tried to bring him up as my own but it is not easy sometimes.*

*As I said before this is my 3rd time inside for being violent towards Sharon. We have argued and I lash out and hit her, each time I say I am sorry and say I won't do it again, and I do mean it, cos Sharon and the kids mean more to me than anything in this world. I can't understand why I hit someone I love so much. I have never hit the kids ever.*

*My father used to beat me up as far back as I can remember, and I remember I once ran to my mom for help, but she just pushed me back to my father who would continued to beat me up. I remember once being tied up and beaten for days. My mum and dad would argue and fight all the time-I have no happy memories with my parents.*

*Each time I have come out of prison I have thought I can control myself and won't do it again, but now I know I can't and need help, before I really hurt her or lose her.*

*I really am desperate for help. I don't know how long I will get, but if I get out how can I get on counselling session. Or if I get time if there is a way of getting help from in here.*

*Thank you for reading this letter, and I hope you can help me in some way, I hope to hear from you soon.*

*Thanks again.*

*Yours sincerely....*

It breaks my heart each time I read this letter, for it reminds me of the sad and often heroic attempts many men have made at getting help for the difficulties they face. Working with perpetrators to change their violent behaviour is still a fairly new concept, with some countries more advanced in this work than others. Even in developed countries such as Britain there are not nearly enough projects to support men in changing their behaviour. Working with women perpetrators is almost non-existent and it is still not acceptable to raise the issue of women's violence in some circles. In less developed countries the work with perpetrators has barely begun. Critics point to the drop-out rate from projects working with men, or argue that men only learn new ways to hurt women. Some of this criticism may be true but perpetrators can and do change; this is what one survivor of domestic violence wrote after her husband had completed the Everyman programme (names have been changed):

*Dear Luke,*

*My husband Cyril has been attending the Everyman Centre for ten months and I have noticed an immense improvement in his temperament.*

*I have had a relationship with Cyril for thirteen years and have been married to him for six of those years.*

*Unfortunately due to his continuing violence I experienced throughout the years I eventually had to leave him as I felt that my life was in danger.*

*On leaving him I sought advice from the local police station. I was given the telephone number of the Everyman Centre. I was not convinced that the counsellors could help him…I kept in contact with my husband by telephone and occasional visits to see if his temperament had changed for the best and I noticed the vast improvement in him.*

*His whole attitude towards life and towards me was more positive and he became more patient, understanding and tolerable towards me and other people.*

*I have since returned to my husband and we are expecting our first baby in September.*

*It is imperative that "Everyman Centre" continues to function so that men with violent behaviour and personal problems can benefit the good work the counsellors can offer them and possibly change their lives to become better people. Obviously the individual will have to be prepared to work hard with the guidance of the counsellor who will enable them to regain self-esteem, respect and fulfilling life in the community.*

*I would like to take this opportunity to thank you and all your colleagues for your work in counselling Cyril. My special thanks goes to Luke.*

*Yours Sincerely....*


No discussion on domestic violence would be complete without a reference to the ones who are directly affected by violence, often termed "victims"; however, this is not a useful concept when someone is fighting to regain self-esteem, so the more positive "survivors" will be used throughout this book.

From my experience of work with survivors I know that they are likely to be looking for solutions to the violence within themselves. Maybe it is something they do that makes the violence happen — after all, they have been told so enough times by the perpetrator. Survivors also feel guilty because they could not stop the violence. They feel shame and are reluctant to tell friends or family members of the abuse. I know many survivors will read this book simply because they want to understand their partner's violence, in order to help them stop the violence. But a word of caution: it is not your job to stop your partner's violence. Perpetrators must accept responsibility for their actions and seek help to stop their violence. It is not helpful for perpetrators to think that the survivor bears some responsibility for their violent behaviour. You may contribute to a bad relationship in many ways but it is the perpetrator's choice to use violence that is the problem. It is not your job to change them, though being supportive of their efforts to change is helpful. Being aware of the reasons for their bad behaviour will help you realize that you are not to blame for their violence. It has nothing to do with you, but with the perpetrator's choice to use violence; although that choice may be limited and influenced by their socialization for violence.

Saying no to violence is important and I have noticed that women who were not subjected to domestic violence as children do not tolerate domestic violence for any length of time. Many have simply moved out of the house at the first incident, often forcing the perpetrator to seek help urgently. Taking action to end the violence early on is important, as the violence is liable to escalate, as explained by *dissonance theory* which argues that once the abuse happens there is an attempt by the perpetrator to justify the action. Once the action has been justified it is more likely to be repeated,[26] putting the survivor at increased risk, and research shows that chronic victims are more likely to sustain serious injury.[27]

Some survivors' tolerance to domestic violence may well have something to do with their early experience of violence. Many were hit as children and told it was "for your own good" or it was "because I love you"; these very confusing messages may be one reason why many survivors suffer up to 35 attacks before calling the police. The belief of some survivors that it is because the perpetrator loves them that he hits them is not uncommon. A study by the World Health Organization found that: "Acceptance of wife-beating was higher among women who had experienced abuse than among those who had not."[28]

Survivors face criticism from everyone for staying in the abusive relationship. Only they can explain why they stay; the options may not be easy for various reasons, such as loving the person, or for cultural or economic considerations. Some are simply too scared to leave the abuser. If survivors want to save the relationship it is useful to undertake some relationship counselling, with a facilitator who can remain objective in helping them find solutions to the problems. This is best done after the perpetrator has had help with their violent patterns of behaviour. Survivors also need help to overcome the effects of a violent relationship. Counselling can be useful to bring about closure in the relationship, especially when children are involved.

After working with one perpetrator for a number of months and speaking with the survivor on the phone I agreed to facilitate a one-off meeting. This is what the survivor wrote after the session. The names have been changed to protect identity.

*Dear Luke,*

*Just a note to thank you for acting as mediator between Martin and myself yesterday. It helped me enormously, I feel as if a weight has been lifted from my shoulders and I was grateful the session helped Martin to accept the fact I couldn't forgive him & intend to carry the divorce proceedings through.*

*I am really pleased he is attending the programme & am glad I made the effort to find out about the organization for him. As I said to both you and Martin I don't want anyone else to go through what I have over the last 7 years.*

*After the last attack I have however lost any respect for Martin. The mere fact that he could hit me while I was holding such a young baby, I find so painful…*

*Who knows, I may in the future like the new non-violent Martin!*

*Once again Luke, many, many thanks for all the help.*

*With kind regards,*
*Susan.*

A word of caution for survivors: this book will help perpetrators but from my experience I know that they work at different paces. Some will take longer than others to get to the place where they will no longer use violence. It is good to have the expectation that their violence will stop immediately but there are no guarantees that this will be the case, so remain hopeful but cautious of the violence and be prepared to move if that seems the safest option.

A place of refuge for survivors is absolutely essential in the strategy for defeating domestic violence and more refuges are needed, but it is not *the* solution to the problem and a better proportion of resources must go towards work with perpetrators to help bring about a permanent solution. One woman, who worked at a refuge, wanted to encourage us in the work with perpetrators after seeing the documentary "Pulling the Punches". This is what she wrote:

*"A co-worker told me that after she had left her violent partner, and became a refuge worker, a few years later she met another woman in the refuge as a result of the same man's violence."*

Politicizing the work with perpetrators is necessary if we are to achieve zero tolerance of domestic violence. Some practitioners approach this work with the view that violence is a problem that resides within individuals, their violence a purely personal, isolated act, a result of their individual "badness"; the solution therefore to ending their violence can only be found through an understanding of their personalities, with little emphasis on the society they live in. Although it is true that every person must be seen as an individual, with unique experiences of life and needing specific attention for his/her particular distresses, we must not underestimate the overall effects of the culture of violence we are subjected to on a daily basis. The roots of domestic violence lie in the oppressive patriarchal societies we live in and real lasting change is only possible by engaging in political activity to end all oppression.

The "zero tolerance" refrain to domestic violence popular in some developed countries is meaningless unless there is zero tolerance to all violence, including state violence of the police, army, penal and mental health system. It has been said often enough that violence breeds violence, and studies show that this is true not only of civilian use of violence but also with the use of state violence. If we ignore violence to children and men-on-men violence, zero tolerance will remain but a pipe dream. As bell hooks puts it: "Women and men must oppose the use of violence as a means of social control in all its manifestations: war, male violence against women, adult violence against children, teenage violence, racial violence, etc. Feminist movement to end violence must be expanded into a movement to end all forms of violence."[29]

Violence is a learned behaviour and the awareness that men have been manipulated to mistreat women in support of patriarchy and socialized to be violent has helped many perpetrators stop their violent behaviour. Some of the men I have worked with over the years have become advocates of ending all forms of violence, and often interrupt violence in other men. One man after completing the Everyman programme wrote:

> I'd like to thank everyone at the Everyman Centre, for all the support and help, also advice they have gave to me during the six months I've been coming to the Everyman Centre, I have most certainly learnt, understood and most of all started to feel, instead of— this course has helped me to understand that others have feelings, fears and problems. I will miss the one-to-one also the group sessions.
>
> My individual counselling was of top Professional Counsel.
>
> I now look forward and hope that I can join the Everyman to help on the phone lines. I now feel I can offer to others that are in the same position that I was. I hope I can continue to grow and use all I've learnt after my duration at the Everyman.

Society can no longer tolerate domestic violence as it has done in the past. Perpetrators have no choice but to change their violent behaviour. You can change! I have changed and most of the perpetrators I have worked with have changed. We can do this together.

Let us begin.

# HOW TO USE THIS BOOK

This is an interactive book, in the sense that you and I get to "work" together. I put myself central to the book, in the role of counsellor for you, the "client" who wants to stop your violent behaviour. For me to be your counsellor I must have your agreement to be my client. I want you to think for a moment about what this will mean for you. It will involve me asking you lots of personal questions, asking you to talk or write about and reflect on experiences you may have never talked about before; asking you to look at the areas of your life that may have been extremely painful, that you would rather be shut away for ever.

For this book to work for you, you must be prepared to look at yourself and face some truths however painful that may be. I need you to commit to being open and honest with your responses to the set *exercises*. Changing attitude and behaviour does not happen overnight, so patience and determination on your part will be required. You must stop to do some thinking/ feeling and sometimes some writing. Feelings of rage, despair, grief and isolation may surface at times when looking at some of the issues. If the feelings are overwhelming this may be a signal that you need support with this. Seeing a counsellor or therapist may be the best way to explore these deep feelings. I cannot be there in person to support your thinking and feeling but having a good cry often helps. If there are feelings of rage having a cushion or pillow to hit will ease the frustration and leave you feeling better. Engaging with the *exercises* is a crucial part of the process and not to be missed. It is best to have a safe place where you can show feelings if you think an exercise may bring up deep feelings. If you can do this with the support of someone you trust and they are really willing to listen to you this would be a great help (there are some helpful tips in the final chapter on how they can best do this). It would be wrong to do any of these exercises with the one you hurt and you must not attempt to involve them in any way. Remember that I am there for you as your counsellor — supporting, non-judgmental and caring of your efforts.

There will be many challenges but I won't expect anything of you I wouldn't do myself. I will be sharing some of my personal experiences so that you get to know and I hope trust me as your counsellor. I cannot be there in person to convey my concern, respect, love, and high expectation of you. But I want you to know that it is there, no matter how hard it gets for you. You have to trust that I will not give up on you. I trust that you want to change and are prepared to work hard for that change. The process will only work for you, if you agree to "work" with me; agree to be my "client". I need that agreement from you. Now! It's decision time! Can I get that agreement from you to be my client?

Thank you! Now we can move on.

You will have to be patient and it is good to remember that what we are attempting here is usually done at the very least over a six-month period, involving many hours of individual and group counselling. There will be a temptation for you to read the book from cover to cover in a short time. That is fine but you should go over it again, taking time to do the exercises and allowing for feelings. Many of you will not have experienced counselling before, so I will briefly describe some **key words and concepts** used to help get you through the book:

**Counselling**. This is the process in which a person is listened to by a counsellor, whose role is to support that person's thinking to help them find solutions to their difficulties. There are different approaches to counselling but all have some element of this. It should not be confused with advice giving.

**Counsellor**. This is a trained person, in one or more of several disciplines, who listens to another person/client with the intention of supporting, giving information and at times challenging their thinking. Often the client is looking for help to change behaviour or attitude that is causing them some difficulty.

**Client**. This is the person seeking help with some difficulty they are experiencing and who has agreed to talk or "work" with a counsellor.

**Individual session.** Time spent with a counsellor talking through difficulties, in confidence, with the counsellor giving their undivided, loving, non-judgmental attention. A typical session lasts for about fifty minutes.

**Group work**. This is a group with facilitator, counsellor or therapist working with them, to support their recovery from hurtful experiences. Group work can be time-limited, is sometimes "closed", admitting no new members, or "open", admitting new members at any stage. Some group work may have more than one facilitator/counsellor, sometimes a male and a female working together. At the Everyman Centre I did ten group-work sessions, one evening a week, lasting two and a half hours each, with a male co-facilitator working with a group of ten men. Some groups run for much longer.

**Oppression**. This refers to the systematic mistreatment of a group of people by the society, or by another group of people who serve as agents of the society with the mistreatment encouraged or/and enforced by the society.

**Liberation** refers to the programme and process of freeing oneself and one's group from oppression.

**Domestic violence** has many definitions, but most involve the use of physical, emotional, financial, psychological or sexual abuse of a woman or man within a relationship.

**Sexism** defines the ideology of male supremacy, of male superiority and of beliefs that sustain and support it. Sexism and patriarchy mutually reinforce one another.

**Gender** is "the cultural definition of behaviour defined as appropriate to the sexes in a given society at a given time. Gender is a set of cultural roles. It is a costume, a mask, a straitjacket in which men and women dance their mutual dance".[1]

**Patriarchy** "in its wider definition means the manifestation and institutionalization of male dominance over women and children in the family and the extension of male dominance over women in society in general. It implies that men hold power in all the important institutions of society and that women are deprived of access to such power. It does not imply that women are either totally powerless or totally deprived of rights influence and resources…. This was a process that took some 2,500 years to develop from approximately 1300 to 600 BC."[2]

**Archaic states**. "These came about at different times in different places throughout the world, in a process by which scattered Neolithic villages became agricultural communities, then urban centres, and finally states. This has been called "the urban revolution" or the "rise of civilization". Archaic states are everywhere characterized by the emergence of property classes and hierarchies. It is the emergence and consolidation of military elites; kingship; the institutionalization of slavery; a transition from kin dominance to patriarchal families".[3]

**Cognitive dissonance theory**. "Basically cognitive dissonance is a state of tension that occurs whenever an individual simultaneously holds two cognitions (ideas, attitudes, beliefs, opinions) that are psychologically inconsistent. Stated differently two cognitions are dissonant if, considering these two cognitions alone, the opposite of one follows from the other.

Because the occurrence of cognitive dissonance is unpleasant, people are motivated to reduce it." One way of reducing cognitive dissonance is by changing one or both cognitions in such a way as to render them more compatible (more consonant) with each other.[4]

**Internalization**. "The internalization of a value or belief is the most permanent, most deeply rooted response to social influence. The motivation to internalise a particular belief is the desire to be right. Thus the reward of the belief is intrinsic. If the person who provides the influence is perceived to be trustworthy and of good judgement, we accept the belief he or she advocates and we integrate it into our own system of values. Once it is part of our system it becomes independent of its source and will become extremely resistant to change".[5]

**Internalized oppression**. When we think and act on the basis of the oppression we face we have internalized it. This is the best tool of the oppressive society. If we agree to and collude in our own oppression the oppressive society does not have to enforce the oppression, we do the job for them. The best way to bring about permanent change is to internalize the desirable values and belief systems and make them our own.

**Oppressive society**. Societies are oppressive because they evolved in that way in the first place, out of oppressive archaic states. Societies are oppressive because there is inequality, and mistreatment to maintain that inequality. Most of us face some kind of oppression in our lives. Young people and older people face oppression because of their age, women face oppression because of their gender, others because of their religion, and so on. Each social group plays its part in keeping oppressive societies functioning; for example, with racism, white people may do the oppressing of Black people; with sexism, men typically do the oppressing of women.

My approach to working with people with violent patterns is grounded mostly in Re-evaluation Counselling, theory and practice. We argue that everyone comes into this world completely good, intelligent, powerful, creative, loving, etc. It is helpful that you have an understanding of how the process works for it to be most effective, briefly put:

**Re-evaluation counselling**. A well defined practice of listening, taking turns to listen, and allowing and assisting emotional release, which enables participants to remove the effects of past hurtful experiences and to think clearly where they had previously been confused.

These are a set of our concepts and beliefs, stated briefly:

1.  We assume that the only source of dysfunction in a human being is an experience of hurt, either physical or emotional, which leaves the information input during that hurt experience in the form of a rigid, compulsive pattern of feeling and behaviour rather than as useful information.

2.  We assume complete recoverability from distress, provided the fore brain is intact.

3.  We set a goal of total function for the human being. We reject any cultural standards of norm and assume that each human being has the capacity to flower and flourish far beyond any currently observable models.

4.  We assume "discharge" is the important and almost the only step in the recovery process that requires outside assistance. By discharge we mean a series of very complex processes that humans go through, which we are not yet in a position to define physiologically. This process can be observed to happen. We concentrate on what we call the dependable outward indications of these processes: tears, trembling, perspiration,

laughter, angry shouting, reluctant but non-repetitive talk, eager talk and, associated with these, the process that is dependably characterized by yawns. There is still much to be learned about these processes but recently scientists have found that the tears of joy are chemically different to the tears for sorrow.

5. We assume that given attainable conditions, discharge becomes spontaneous.

6. We understand that the precondition for discharge is the division of the client's free attention approximately equally between the distress on which discharge is being sought and material contradictory to the distress.

7. The results of discharge are the dissolution of the compulsive pattern, a freeing of the compulsive pattern, a freeing of the frozen intelligence and the conversion of the pattern to useful, available and flexible information.[6]

**Patterns.** Ways of thinking or behaving that may be rooted in past hurtful experiences.

**Re-stimulation.** To be reminded of a past hurtful experience and to act on the basis as if the hurt was currently being experienced.

**Discharge.** A process inherent to humans, which heals emotional damage from distressful incidents. Outward signs of this process include animated talking, crying, trembling, yawning, expressions of anger and laughter.

**Commitments.** This is a tool used in co-counselling to assist discharge. Sometimes used in group work or with a counsellor. Like "affirmations" you can use them by yourself; take time to notice any feelings that you may have as you do.

One of the greatest problems facing projects with perpetrators is the drop-out rate. Some projects have devised "contracts" to help overcome this problem. I want you to "commit" to seeing the programme through. Some perpetrators want to change for their partners and if the relationship comes to an end they lose interest in completing the programme. Make no mistake: you have to do this for yourself! Not for Jane or Juliet or John, but just for yourself; because you deserve a better life. You cannot have a good life while you are hurting people, so I want you to commit to seeing the program through. You have had a lifetime of one kind of attitude and behaviour and it will take more than a few hours to change them, so don't you ever give up on your attempts to stop your violent behaviour.

Some attempts by projects working at changing men's violent behaviour may have failed simply because men have been coerced into joining and staying in their programme. No one can force you to change your attitude: you may be forced to change your behaviour at times, but if you don't change your attitude, the behaviour will reassert itself when it feels safe to do so. It will help for you to approach this project as something that you want to do *for you*, not to please anyone else, but just because you want better for yourself.

**Decision**. Making a decision to change and having the courage and commitment to get you through this book will help you stop your violence. You have to decide to change. No one can make you change, not by force, coercion nor bribery. Only by a decision from you is real change possible. You will have to keep making that decision to change for a while, so every day you wake the first thing to remind yourself of is the decision to stop using violence. Try making this "decision to stop using violence" commitment daily:

*"I make a decision never again to use violence against anyone, especially not against ----, and I will repeat this decision as often as is necessary to free my life completely from violent behaviour."*

Remember you are trying to undo a pattern of behaviour that has perhaps been with you for many years. It will help for you to write this commitment down and display it in places where you will see it regularly so that you are constantly reminded. Remember, only you can make that decision to change work; and it helps if you have a positive attitude in approaching the problem. If you tell yourself you cannot do a task there is a very good chance you will fail at it; making a decision that you can will help. Be aware that when you make a decision to stop your violence you are deciding to stand against oppression. The oppressive society depends on our acceptance of the use of violence, if all else fails. When you decide not to use violence you refuse to collude with the oppressive society.

Taking responsibility for your violence is an important first step to recovery; unless you take responsibility you will never stop your violent behaviour. If you are not responsible for your actions then you have no power to change them. When you use violence it is because you "choose" to do so – although this choice is based on hurtful experiences and socialization for violence that makes you feel you have no other choice. You may feel that you had no choice, but you actually did; you could have walked away from the situation, you could have screamed, cried, laughed, run or whatever. You did not have to hit. You made that choice. You only have to notice that after choosing violence you then decided carefully on where to target your blows, whether to attack the head, face or body. Your muscles do not move without a command from your brain (except for a few reflex actions, such as the knee-jerk or sneezing).

Your decision to use violence is dependent on many factors but there is nothing inherent in you that *makes* you violent. You have learnt "violent patterns of behaviour" because of your socialization for violence, but it is not you - this is something that was imposed upon you and you can un-learn it. Any notion of "she/he made me do it" must be got rid of completely. Just as no one can force you to change your attitude similarly no one can make you hit. It is your decision, however premeditated or split-second, it is your action. Only you can stop it!

The decision to use violence is entirely yours, no matter how distressed you were at the time. You must accept that you are responsible for your actions. Any attempt to blame someone or something else will make it difficult, if not impossible, for you to change. This is an important step in your recovery so I say again: if you are not responsible for your actions, how can you stop them? You can't stop doing something you weren't responsible for making happen in the first place. We may have to keep returning to this, as I know from my work with perpetrators it is hard for them to accept responsibility for hurting someone they love; it does not sit well with them. Besides, many of you will have been affected by the thinking that the violence is something inside you that you have no control over, the genes, the blood, the skin, nature or something. We will return to this discussion in Chapter Two.

There is good reason for this reluctance to accept responsibility for your violence, according to social scientist's "dissonance theory" of human behaviour, as explained above. In this case the two cognitions, (a) *I am a good man/woman* and (b) *I have hurt someone*, are psychologically inconsistent. The theory argues that we try to reduce dissonance whenever it occurs, as it makes us uncomfortable, hence the avoidance of taking responsibility. One of the easy ways out of this discomfort is to blame the other person; "she/he made me do it", so you don't have to feel bad (dissonance). This is partly action to protect your ego, which does not like being hurt and with good reason. Apparently we don't function well when our egos are hurt and I definitely want your ego in good shape to help get you through the challenges of stopping your violent behaviour. Accepting responsibility now for your violent actions will reap greater rewards for your ego later on.

**Empathy**. The ability to understand what another person is feeling is inherent to all humans unless they suffered some very specific brain damage. Some people have been badly hurt and then prevented from showing any feelings about the hurt. If someone gets hurt and is denied the opportunity to heal from the experience, sometimes simply by being listened to, they are left with the distress and often act out the painful experience on others. If when someone gets hurt they have the opportunity to talk about it and can show how they really feel, then they are able to heal from those hurts, in what we argue is a natural healing process of the body. For example, if someone was hit a lot as a child and no healing was allowed to take place there is a pull for them to act out this distress on their own or other children. Given the opportunity to talk and feel about those past hurtful experiences can help the abused to recover from them however long ago they happened.

Developing empathy is crucial in ending violent behaviour as there is evidence that the more empathy a person has the less likely they are to be aggressive.[7] It is important that you are able to understand what it feels like to be hurt by someone. To understand what it feels like to be frightened every time you see someone, or hear their raised voice, at the thought of *them* returning home, the fear that you could be hurt at any time, to feel powerless and what that does to your self-esteem and confidence as a person.

When humans are hurting physically or emotionally it is natural to want to cry. When boys are conditioned to repress feelings with "come on, big boys don't cry", their emotional repertoire is much more limited than that of girls, and so is their ability to empathize. This systematic interruption prevents the natural healing process of the body from taking place, and is responsible for much of the bad things that men do. Women too have had this process interrupted but to a lesser extent. Reclaiming the ability to express feelings is part of the healing process. I will encourage you whenever any feelings such as sadness, rage, joy or hurt come up during the course of this book, for you to just go right ahead and express them.

**Self-esteem.** Having high self-esteem is important in overcoming violent behaviour as research shows that most perpetrators suffer from low self-esteem. Without a doubt, we came into this world with high self-esteem as babies, full of confidence, powerful and intelligent, but it was not long before our confidence was undermined by the adults around us as we began to explore the environment– for our own safety/good we are often told, or just out of sheer ignorance. Depending on the extent to which we have been put down, discouraged and mistreated we could grow up with our self-esteem in tatters. Recalling those early experiences will help you recognize where you have been hurt. Taking time to express some feelings of grief or rage will help you overcome the effects of the mistreatment. Understanding how your self-esteem was undermined will help you work out a strategy to overcome it. For instance, if you were made to feel that you were ugly, looking in the mirror daily and acknowledging your beauty will help you to be more accepting of yourself. We are all unique, no one looks exactly or even quite like you do, so who decides what constitutes beauty? You can decide that you are the most beautiful, by the standards you set.

Everyday affirmations can help contradict the mistreatment we endured as children. We all came into this world completely good, intelligent, and powerful but being mistreated in some way makes us forget that. Try asking yourself some of the following questions every day and replying in the affirmative (even if you can't believe it yet) and see what a difference it makes to how you feel about yourself. It works much better if you can get someone you trust to ask the questions and pay you attention; if this is not possible you can begin with asking yourself: "How good am I?" The answer must always be in the affirmative as "completely good"; and remember that this is true of you. You are inherently good and any bad behaviour is because of the patterns you have learnt as a result of the mistreatment and misinformation you were subjected to as a child. Try remembering the times when you knew you were completely good and hold on to those memories. Feelings may come up during this exercise, just give time to feel them and allow the healing to begin. Repeat this exercise by substituting "How good?" with, for example, "How intelligent?" "How beautiful?" "How caring?" "How loving?" The answer must always be in the affirmative - "completely caring", for example.

**Awareness-raising.** Being aware of the oppressive society we live in is crucial in ending domestic violence. We cannot end domestic violence without challenging the structures that support and depend on the use of violence. The oppressive patriarchal societies we live in rely on a number of key oppressions, to "divide and rule", for its survival. We get separated in every way and the oppression of women is one of the oldest kinds sustaining the oppressive society; but all oppressions are intrinsically intertwined, and it makes no sense arguing over a hierarchy of oppression. Men cannot be liberated while women remain oppressed - we cannot end any oppression without unravelling the others. Every excuse to confuse and separate us has been used - race, sex, class, age, sexuality, size, religion, disability, etc.

We may find ourselves in the role of oppressed and oppressor at the same time. For example, adults may be oppressed because of class or gender while oppressing others because of race or age. We cannot end oppression if we do not give up our oppressor roles.

The use of violence is essential in perpetuating the oppressive society. This reliance on violence makes it difficult for the oppressive state to create the conditions necessary to end all violence. The oppressive state may tinker with changes to end domestic violence - for example, by proposing longer prison sentences - but these measures often only breed more violence. Defeating domestic violence will require internalizing a new value system that is against all oppression, and especially with "zero tolerance" for all violence, including state violence. This is why it is important to have an open mind as you progress through the book as many long-held beliefs will be challenged. Being aware of the root causes of violent behaviour will help empower you to take responsibility for changing your attitude and behaviour, and help bring about a more equal society.

**Individual sessions**

I can't be there for you in person, but imagine that I am - that I am there giving you my full non-judgmental attention in a loving way. I will challenge any attitude or behaviour of yours that is contributing to your violence. I will not blame you but support you to make the changes necessary to end your violence. You will have feelings come up from time to time. I want you to know that it is fine to have them and that I welcome them.

By using your imagination and intelligence it will not be too difficult to do the exercises. You will sometimes be asked to write "counter essays" (a technique used by social scientists to help people change their attitude and behaviour). If writing is difficult, you will have to think and use your imagination to talk to me about it. It takes a long time and lots of misinformation and mistreatment for patterns of behaviour that are hurtful to you and to others to be installed. Undoing the harm will take a little time and determination from you.

The individual sessions are so that we get to work with the specifics of your hurts and your difficulties; no two situations are identical, we are all different people and need tailor-made solutions to our problems. Having said that, some generalizations can be made about domestic violence and I will be using my experience of working with perpetrators to cover some of the issues that come up regularly, with the hope that I will cover your particular issue.

When doing the exercises it would be good for you to create a space where you are able to express your feelings; where you can cry if you want to or have a cushion to hit if feelings of rage surface. People get confused about hitting cushions sometimes. It is not a rehearsal for violence but an exercise to help you safely get rid of the angry feelings without hurting anyone.

It takes courage to face your weaknesses and to challenge and change them. We don't like to hear and see things that conflict with our deeply held beliefs or wishes. This book is going to challenge many things in you, but don't you back off from the work you have to do here. It takes a lot of courage to change any behaviour. My decision as your counsellor is to stick with you, no matter how hard it gets. I will not back off from your pain, or stop believing in your goodness. I will not be afraid of your angry feelings. I will challenge all of your thinking and behaviour that make domestic violence a reality. I will keep respecting and loving you no matter what your story is; I want you to know that I will not require anything of you that I would not do myself. Let us begin.

**First session:** "What brings you here?" This question often brings up all the memories of the incident. Take time to answer and to notice any feelings that may surface as a result of reviewing the incident. If there are lots of feelings expressed (sometimes by crying) it is a good indication that you are ready to begin the healing process. It is important that you feel about the things you do that cause pain. I encourage you to be open and honest with me in your sessions for it will help you to change your behaviour. In every session I ask about your feelings. This is to get you accustomed to thinking about and expressing your feelings and it helps me understand what is going on in your life at the moment. I am sorry that you have done these things; they are not acceptable. You can change this behaviour, by making the decision to change and keep working at it.

Many perpetrators try to "minimize" the violence they do. The perpetrators who have been able to make rapid progress with stopping their violence are the ones who are able to face up to their actions. If you can face the fact that your actions caused pain it will help you to stop your violence. To talk of it being "just a slap" or "just a push" or "just words" is to try to minimize your actions and not accept responsibility. Being in denial will not help the process, what may seem like a "just…" to you is hurtful to another person physically and emotionally, so don't minimize your acts of violence as you tell your story.

> **Exercise: Begin the healing.** Stop to think and feel about your last act of violence, remembering not to lay blame and to allow for feelings.

If you are living with the one you hurt, you need to think about how you are going to make the situation safe for them.

These are some strategies for you to use immediately:

1. No Denial. Talk about your violence to the people that matter. Tell your siblings, in-laws, friends, parents, family and children. Getting the abuse out in the open will help you to stop. Let these people know that you are working hard to change this behaviour.

2. Think about the things that "trigger" your violence and avoid them. For example, this could be a "critical" pattern - always finding things or ways to criticize your partner. You must stop this straight away.

3. Make a decision to stop your violent behaviour. Using the commitments/affirmations on a daily basis can help break this pattern of behaviour.

4. Become an advocate against domestic violence; tell people how wrong you think it is and interrupt other perpetrators justifying their actions if you can.

5. Learn to love yourself. Most perpetrators have been deeply hurt themselves and have low self-esteem; work at building this up. Think about the things that make you feel positive about yourself and remind yourself that you are inherently good.

6. Take "time out": This is a technique for you to implement immediately to help break the pattern of violence. It is simply a chance for you and your partner to have a cooling-off period. For it to work you must both agree to abide by the rules. First, you decide on a "stop" sign; this could be with the hand, body, sound or simply the word "stop". Once the agreed stop sign is activated by you or by your partner, you must abide to a "six-foot" rule; you step well back from your partner and do not enter that space until the agreed time has elapsed. You will have discussed this agreed cooling-off period at a calmer moment and agree to abide by it. You

will also have agreed how and where time out should be spent. Maybe you have to leave the room or house for a short period (half an hour or so). You must return at the precise time agreed and if necessary ask for another *time out*.

This *time out* is not a time to take any mind-altering substances, but an opportunity for you to clear your head and regain composure. Remind yourself of your decision not to use violence, repeat the commitment against violence (see below). You will only hate yourself for going back on your word. It's not worth it. It is the time to reflect on your behaviour. I know you will be feeling really bad about yourself. There may be angry feelings, guilty feelings, hating myself, type of feelings. You must let go of those feelings and try to remember that you are inherently good; that you would not use violence if you were not mistreated or seen violence as a young person. Try remembering the times when you had a sense of your own goodness. Domestic violence can never be justified; no matter what the circumstances. You have a choice. You are not inherently bad, just behaving badly. In spite of the violence, you are a good person deep down inside and you know it. It's just sometimes hard to keep holding on to that good person. Your partner would not be in a relationship with you if they did not see that good person at times. You must go back to the times when the relationship was going well and try to remember what it felt like. You may also want to think of any pleasant memories you have of holiday, food, party etc to help change your mood.

Some perpetrators who would not use violence when sober will do so under the influence of mind-altering substances, as this gives them something else to blame for the violence. If this applies, you must get help with giving up the substance, as it is difficult to "work" with anyone who is addicted to mind-altering substances. Anything that gets in the way of you being in touch with your true feelings will slow the process of change, if not make it impossible. If you are using drugs of any kind you must have a plan on how you are going to give them up. You can best do this with some expert support. If you cannot get help with the addiction from a specialist project then it may be useful to read the chapter on defeating addictions now.

**Session time:** So you hurt your partner because you were angry and frustrated - if only she/he had not said or done that something that annoyed you. You may have felt hurt and angry but that does not give you the right to abuse your partner in any way. It was not their fault that you "lost it". It was your choice to hit and the sooner you can accept that, the better for you. Although it is true that the type of socialization you received may have limited your choice, it was still your decision to use violence. You can now make a decision never to use violence again. Keep repeating the commitment below on a daily basis. Try saying it aloud placing emphasis on some key words for *you* and inserting the name of the person you hurt.

*"I make a decision never again to use violence against anyone, especially not against -----, and I will repeat this decision as often as is necessary to free my life completely from violent behaviour."*

**Exercise: Developing empathy.** Think/ talk or write about all the things you think the one you hurt is going through.

**Session time:** That you are feeling bad about yourself and guilty for the hurt you have caused is understandable. What you have done is unacceptable; I am really sorry you have hurt your partner, but to wallow in guilty feelings is only trying to get sympathy for yourself. What is required is that you take action to change your violent behaviour. Guilt is a wasted emotion, for no amount of guilty feelings will change anything; the sooner you give up on guilt, the earlier we can move on to taking decisive action for change.

You would not hurt anyone if you did not experience violent behaviour in the first place. Let us take some time to look at what it was like for you as a young one. I want you to tell me about your childhood experiences of violence. Go right back in time to your earliest memories. Remember, this is not about blaming anyone, but being in denial about any mistreatment you received will not help you. Most of us will have been hit or seen violence; it is important to think and talk about that and to notice any feelings that may come up as you do. I am sorry that you were hurt, it never should have happened. If the violence you perpetuate is emotional, notice how this was done to you and how you pass this on to your partner.

**Exercise: Healing the hurts.** Think/talk or write about any violence you experienced as a child, and pay attention to any feelings you may have.

**Session time:** Maybe your partner has left and you feel at a loss and desperately want them back. You want them to know how sorry you are and want to show how much you love them, assuring them that this will never happen again. How many times has this happened? How many times have you broken that promise? I trust that you have made genuine efforts to stop your violence by yourself, but in my experience, those efforts have often failed. It is good that you are now seeking help. You now have a much better chance to stop your violence, but you can't expect your partner to believe this straight away. Why should they believe you this time?

You will have to be patient. A separation may be a good thing for both of you right now. I know this is difficult as all your energy is going towards wanting to make things better. You feel insecure and your "control patterns" will be trying to take charge of the situation. You feel you will lose the relationship if you are separated. Your partner being away feels as if you're losing control of the situation and you can't bear that. You're getting desperate. You have to slow down. Your actions have created this situation. You may be able to save the relationship yet, but there are two people involved here and the other person may want something different.

Face the fact that the relationship may be over. Sometimes too much damage has already been done to the relationship and your partner may have already moved on; you have to accept this. You cannot coerce or force anyone to have a relationship with you. It just won't work. If you are still living together, it is a good idea to decide not to argue or fight over anything that recently "triggered" violence, and remember to use time-out if you feel you are losing control.

Your violence may have cost you this relationship, but you have to ensure that you have used violence for the last time. You can do this by staying the course of the book; you are doing this for yourself, not just to save the relationship. It would be good if that happened, if that is what you and the survivor want; but make no mistake, you must change this behaviour for yourself, so that you have a better life.

> **Exercise: Relationship-building** Think/talk or write about your relationship and what it means to you. What do you have to change to make it work?

Much of the violence men use is a result of their socialization for violence but the sexism and control patterns of behaviour are also significant. The arguments may have been about "her" not cooking the dinner on time or well enough, or not keeping the place clean, or talking to the wrong person and so on. You have to ask yourself, what can I do to make the situation easier?

Some of women's violence is also about controlling behaviour. It may be about anything, from him staying out late, to watching sport, to using mind-altering substances, to the friends she/he keeps. Insecurity is usually not too far away. There may be feelings of jealousy or not trusting. Whatever the excuse for the violence, socialization for violence plays a huge part, as most perpetrators have been hit or exposed to domestic violence as children.

Now that the individual sessions are over, we will continue with the work of stopping violence in groups, so a little about group work before we begin.

**Group work**

The isolation you feel in trying to end your violence is not surprising. In every piece of patterned behaviour that we carry, there is a bit of isolation attached, because there was no one there at the time we were hurting to give the attention we needed to heal. You are not alone in this endeavour to end your violent behaviour. I am there and there are millions of perpetrators in the world trying to stop their violence. Imagine a group of supporters just for you, encouraging your every attempt to change; this is what "group work" is all about.

Often the groups I worked with were made up of men of different religion, race, class and age, and all of these issues are addressed in the group. Working-class men are often portrayed as violent; this is not a helpful stereotype and may contribute to the fact that working-class people are twice as likely to be abused or be abuser.[8] In the same way, the stereotyping of black men as violent has led to many black men internalizing the stereotype and acting it out on the people closest to them. It results in much of the "black on black" violence so prevalent today. Issues of racism and "classism" must be addressed in the work to defeat domestic violence. To do justice to these issues would take volumes and may be more appropriate for another book; besides, these issues do not arise in the same way when working on your own.

I hope you have completed all the exercises in this section and that you are beginning to feel better in yourself. There is some evidence that social learning can make a difference to violent behaviour and this must be utilized in the struggle to end domestic violence.[9] We will now move on to the group-work *awareness-raising* sessions, which constitute the rest of the book, and I hope you will stay completely engaged with me in this.

# CHAPTER ONE

...........................

# THE ROOTS OF
# DOMESTIC VIOLENCE

There is nothing new about domestic violence, it has been around at least for as long as we have recorded history and its roots may well lie in the distresses of our ancestors in their fight for survival. In prehistoric times, women were abducted for their childbearing ability by "other" clans desperately trying to increase their population to enhance their chances of survival in a hostile environment. One imagines that violence and threats of violence would have been used to keep women from returning to their clan once abducted. This scenario, repeated many times over thousands of years by men, could be partially responsible for the installation of patterns of violence towards women, passed on from one prehistoric generation to the next. As patriarchy became entrenched, the subordination of women was firmly enshrined in law. Men literally held in their hands the right to life or death of women and children and were encouraged and coerced by patriarchal society to dominate women.[1]

The ruling elite, who established the first archaic states, laid the foundations for today's oppressive societies, foundations that were deeply flawed from the very beginning, like the foundations of buildings built on a rubbish dump. After a while, such buildings begin to subside as poisonous gases seep from the rotting dump. The occupants of the houses are slowly being poisoned[2] and the structure of the houses begins to collapse. Eventually, the poisonous gases combine to cause an explosion, destroying what was built on poor foundations. Our societies face a somewhat similar situation because of the inherently oppressive nature of the relationships that hold it together.

Defeating domestic violence will mean defeating patriarchy, because much of the difficulties we face stem from this corrupt system supporting a monopoly of power by men over women. During the formation of patriarchy women were subordinated based on their gender but men were also oppressed: because of their greater muscular strength and skill at fighting, men were constantly coerced into fighting wars that sometimes lasted for scores or even hundreds of years. It seemed that all men did was fight, or prepare to fight. As a result the socialization for violence has been relentless for men and continues today regardless of the fact that our survival may no longer depend on our fighting skills but on our ability to make peace.

For some modern states the rule of patriarchy is now not so obvious, or is it as crude as it used to be, but the system is nevertheless alive and well in most countries. In ancient times women were seen as commodities and often married off into other clans, as a way of reducing the threat of war, or for settling disputes, a practice that has not entirely died out in some countries. For example, it was recently reported in Pakistan how "five girls, aged between two and five were given as compensation to the family of a murdered man."[3]

Much of the problem of male violence is rooted in the philosophies and socialization crucial to maintain the oppressive society. "The patriarchal mode of thought is so built into our mental processes that we cannot exclude it unless we make ourselves consciously aware of it, which always means a special effort".[4] This is the task facing us: to raise our consciousness to a level where we can see the oppression if we are to defeat it. Patriarchy demands that men be in control; if they must use violence to achieve that end, then it is a necessary evil. Society has propagated this viewpoint for a long time and it has affected most of us.

The belief that "might is right" and that "a man's home is his castle" has infected most of the world and provides cover for violence in the home. There is some small shift in attitude in some places about these "castles" but it will take time for these attitudes to change in a substantial way to really make a difference. It is still largely believed by most of the world that a man can do as he pleases in his home and that the state will ignore it, even if that involves the worst forms of mistreatment to the occupants of the house.

Not so long ago in Britain, the police often took no action when called to a house where a woman was being abused, because it was "only a domestic". Now, although they are required to take action when called, not all the forces respond in the same way. Figures in the UK show that the police make an arrest in only 52 per cent of domestic violence cases and the arrest rate varies from 9 per cent to 86 per cent across 29 police forces. This inconsistent reaction to domestic violence is not surprising, given that some officers believe the notion that domestic violence is a personal matter and that men are free to do as they please in their homes.

Domestic violence is never acceptable no matter what the situation. The notion that the use of violence is acceptable must be challenged. Men especially, have to overcome centuries of conditioning that encouraged violence to women. In her book *The Creation of Patriarchy*, Gerda Lerner lays bare the way the subordination of women was established. She points out that during the middle of the second millennium, prostitution was a well-established likely occupation for the daughters of the poor and the sexual regulation of women intensified during this period. The state wanted to be able to distinguish "respectable women" from prostitutes. This was to be achieved by the veiling of women. Only "respectable" women were allowed to wear a veil. If a prostitute was found wearing a veil she was punished. The law states:

> "he who has seen a harlot veiled must arrest her, produce witnesses (and) bring her to the palace tribunal; they shall not take her jewellery away (but) the one who arrested her may take her clothing; they shall flog her fifty (times) with staves (and) pour pitch on her head".[5]

Men were well and truly set up to be the "agents" of oppression of women in the interest of patriarchy. It is heartening to note that not all men rushed forward to collude in oppressing women. Lerner points to evidence which shows that if it could be proved that a man knew someone who broke the law on veiling and did not report her he was subjected to punishment:

> "If a seignior has seen a harlot veiled and has let her go without bringing her to the palace tribunal they shall flog that seignior fifty times with staves; they shall pierce his ears, thread them with a cord, and tie it at his back, and he shall do the work of the king for one full month."[6]

As time passed, these forms of brutal punishment to men and women were gradually outlawed, but some of these worse elements are re-emerging in some countries. Change is slow, and in most countries domestic violence is still not considered a crime. It was not so long ago that men were permitted lawfully to beat their wives in most developed countries. In the UK just over 100 years ago it was legal for a man to beat his wife with a stick provided it was no fatter than his thumb — hence the "rule of thumb" as it is known in law today. In the year 2001 a man could still legally beat his wife in Arkansas, USA, provided it was no more than once a month.[7] Many countries still have laws on their statute books that make it legal for a man to beat his wife. An appeal court in Dubai recently ruled that a husband has a right to beat his wife: "To discipline her; provided he does not damage her bones or deform her body." She could however demand a divorce if her husband "injures her, either by word or action".[8]

In the struggle against domestic violence it is important that there is protection by law, but laws alone will not stop domestic violence; a deep permanent change in attitude is necessary. This can best be achieved by the "internalization" of a different value or belief system, as argued by Elliot Aronson:

> Internalization is the most powerful response to social influence precisely because your motivation to be right is a powerful and self-sustaining force that does not depend upon constant surveillance in the form of agents of reward or punishment, as does compliance...[9]

Stopping violent behaviour demands that we reject the notion of male supremacy that is the foundation of patriarchy. It requires that we work to bring about changes in society and ourselves to achieve a society that treats everyone with respect and dignity. The state may legislate for these changes but it is only by our commitment to change behaviour that we can help bring about the kind of society where we all live in peace and harmony.

The *zero tolerance* to domestic violence advocated in many developed countries is a starting point. This, however, requires zero tolerance to all violence. We cannot hope to end domestic violence while we ignore state violence or violence to children and elders in the home. The changes in legislation protecting women from violence in some countries are to be welcomed, but they are still only tinkering with the solutions to bring about an end to this scourge on society. If our leaders continue to rely on wars to settle political differences, men will always be socialized to be violent. Real solutions involve outlawing all forms of violence and teaching an ethos of non-violence.

A definition of domestic violence that is inclusive is needed if we are to achieve the challenge of a *zero tolerance*. This is the definition I work with:

> *Domestic violence is any form of physical, sexual, emotional, psychological or financial abuse perpetrated in or outside the home on parents, children, men or women by a family member or someone with a history of intimate or close relationship with the family.*

Domestic violence is often physical – usually a punch or a slap, often a push, kick or stab, and more recently the use of weapons such as guns. Threats are used as a way to remind and to frighten. This could be anything: a word, a look, a movement, breaking or throwing of objects punching of walls, etc. Psychological violence usually involves derogatory language used to abuse and undermine the confidence of the survivor. Emotional violence might involve other family members, pets or issues that cause pain and distress to another person. Financial abuse takes the form of withholding, taking away or controlling money.

Getting to the root causes of domestic violence is important in ending it. To help perpetrators change there has to be an understanding of the reasons for their violence. In my work with perpetrators, I have found three major contributory factors:

**1. Hit as children.** Most of the perpetrators I have worked with were hit as children. When children are hit and told, "its' for your own *good*", they learn that it is acceptable to use violence to achieve an end result, "*good*". Some of the most violent perpetrators I have worked with had experienced the worst kinds of mistreatment as children, including sexual and physical abuse. Those who were not so badly mistreated but were hit in a more controlled way tended to be more controlled in their use of violence. This does not mean that all adults who have been hit as children will become perpetrators, but the likelihood of them using violence is much higher than with those who have not been hit. Being hit is not the only factor; other socializing factors are also at work reinforcing the earlier socialization, such as peer violence, addiction to violent movies, television and video games.

Contrary to what some believe, perpetrators do not use the fact that they were hit as children as an excuse for their violence. I have found that many perpetrators are at first reluctant to accept that the violence they experienced as children could possibly be a factor in their own use of violence. Many state that the beatings they received "did me no harm" or that they had done "something to deserve it". These same perpetrators hit their partners, and try to "minimize" the violence and excuse it by saying that she/he did "something to deserve it"; and still they find it hard to see a connection with the violence meted out to them in childhood.

Such denial is understandable, since we generally love our parents/ care givers and don't want to accept that the smacks or beatings they subjected us to may have done any harm. Professor Murray A. Straus, who has researched violence for over 30 years, found that "for both men and women, the more physical punishment a respondent experienced as a child, the higher the probability of assaulting a spouse".[10] Being in denial is not useful when trying to overcome the effects of mistreatment. Accepting that the violence experienced in childhood is part of the problem opens the way for healing and a change in attitude to take place. When children are hit they learn that the use of violence is acceptable - even if only in certain circumstances. Once they accept that violence can be tolerated, we set them up to become perpetrators or victims of violence. We will look at this some more in Chapter Five.

**2. Sexist attitudes**. That is, men holding the view that they are superior to women and their needs are more important than women's, that they are the head of the family and have the right to exercise authority over women and children. If women don't do as they are told such men feel their authority is being undermined. Men have been encouraged in this viewpoint for centuries and many come to think of it as the "natural" way for gender relations. Many believe that women's role is to service men's needs and that *their* needs are more important than women's. Most of the men I counselled believed and behaved as though they were responsible for "their" woman. They believed their partner's behaviour, good or bad, reflected on them - as though they held responsibility for their partner's actions. They saw nothing wrong in taking action to correct any behaviour they did not like - and often that action meant using violence.

**3. Control patterns**. Men have been conditioned - some argue predisposed genetically - to take charge, to lead. Men do this all the time in their relationships without even being aware of it; for example, they tend to dominate and control conversations. Some men hit their partners because she "did not do as she was told". It could be about ironing the clothes, cooking the meal, talking to someone they did not approve of, getting something wrong or right, in fact it could be anything. Much of their violence was directed at correcting behaviour they did not approve.

Women perpetrators also have these deep control patterns and use violence to enforce their wishes where they have the power to do so.

Most of us as young ones will have received some kind of punishment for not "doing as we were told". The list of things we were not allowed is likely to have been exceedingly long, often depending on the list that our parents/carers had as children. As children we get told how to sit, dress, eat, talk, walk, when, how long, how fast, what to think or not think, what to like or not like. The ways in which you were "punished" as a child may well influence the way you perpetrate domestic violence. For example, if you had money or affection withdrawn as punishment you are likely to use these methods in the abuse of your partner. If you were berated, embarrassed/humiliated and isolated, had affection and care withdrawn you are more likely to use psychological and emotional abuse. Being aware of the controlling behaviour is the first step in ending it.

Talking about your violence is crucial in overcoming it. I promised you wouldn't have to do anything I wouldn't do, but it would not be right for me to go into too much detail here, as I wish to protect the privacy of my ex-wife.

**My story: As perpetrator**
It seems such a long time ago, yet the memory of the time I slapped my wife remains very fresh. I hit her hard with an open hand, drawing blood from her nose. As I recall the incident and think of the scene, tears come to my eyes even though this happened over 25 years ago. I was really broken-hearted and disappointed in myself for hurting her.

My life hit a real low after my violence. I felt bad about myself and slipped into a depression that I could not lift myself out of for weeks. Looking back on it, I find that the *dissonance* created as a result of my actions is not surprising. My dad always cautioned us not to hit girls, saying: "Men who hit women are cowards." As a result of this conditioning I avoided fights with girls at school and grew up disapproving of men who hit women. Hitting my wife was against what I had been brought up to believe in.

Weeks after hitting my wife I eventually sought help and fortunately found a co-counsellor to help me. Soon into counselling, when I came to the realization that I had hit my wife mainly because of my socialization for violence, I made a decision always to interrupt domestic violence if I saw it happening, even if simply by getting my body in the way. I was to be tested on this decision sooner and more often than I had imagined, but more on that later.

**Lessons:**

I can see where the socialization by my father was crucial in stopping me from being violent to women for a long time. I felt I would be belittling myself to have a fight with a girl at school, and I worked hard to avoid any possibility of this happening. Being socialized to believe that hitting women was wrong and yet doing it created a great deal of dissonance for me. One way of reducing dissonance is to justify the action. This is what most perpetrators do, but I was so blatantly wrong in the circumstances that led to the violence that there was no way I could justify my actions. As a result, the discomfort I felt forced me to seek help.

Going back over the incident in my mind, I recognize how the socialization for violence took control over any rational thinking, once the "trigger" was activated in my brain. I hated being called "stupid" when I was younger and it almost always led to a fight if someone made out that I was. I was frustrated and angry long before the incident that triggered my violence. So when my wife looked at me as if to say that I was stupid, I "lost" it for a moment and reacted in the way I had been accustomed to doing. I have had to do a lot of work on this area of my life to change that pattern of behaviour.

It is important to recognize the things in you that "trigger" your violent acts, so that you can take steps to "block" the trigger from operating. For instance, if you are male and claim that your partner not "doing as she was told" is a reason for your violence, you must first examine the sexist assumption in this statement. What gives you the right to dictate to a woman what she must or must not do? You need to look back to your childhood experiences to see what happened to you if you did not do as "you were told". If violence was done to you in this context there is a pull for you to act out that behaviour when you are in a similar situation. Making a decision to give up controlling behaviour will help eliminate the trigger.

> **Exercise: Facing your violence.** Time to stop and think/talk about your violence in detail. Try to write down your story and don't hold back on any feelings that surface. In telling your story, remember not to blame anyone for your violence. What do you learn about your behaviour from this exercise?

I hope you were able to have a good cry as you recounted your acts of violence; it is part of the healing process. Do not worry if you couldn't cry, as for some of us the conditioning to not cry is very deep. You have not lost this ability but it will take a little time. Many men I have worked with could not remember the last time they had cried and some were going back twenty years. Some women too have been affected in this way but generally tears have been more acceptable and accessible for women. Give yourself permission to cry; when the safety is there, and the tears will come naturally. Just be open to it happening and allow the tears whenever you feel like it; it is part of the healing process.

There is nothing wrong in having angry feelings. You may well have reason to be angry, but that does not give you the right to use violence. It is better to let your partner know when you are angry by simply telling them that you are angry; not going "over the top" by trying to terrify them with your voice or actions. Using abusive and derogatory language to your partner when angry makes it more likely that you will use violence. You must stop this behaviour if there is to be any chance of stopping your violence.

If you use other kinds of abuse, whether emotional, financial, or sexual, you need to talk about it. Writing down your experiences will help; the more ways you express your thinking and feelings the better. Whatever form of abuse you use is likely to have been learnt from your childhood experiences and can be unlearnt in the same way as with physical violence. Understanding how you learnt violent patterns of behaviour will help you unlearn them. Recognizing the things that trigger your violence will help you avoid them. You may have more than one "trigger"; you will have to examine your behaviour to discover these.

**Exercise: Accepting responsibility.** What triggered your last act of violence? List the things that cause you frustration in your relationship. Think of ways to change or resolve those issues with your partner.

Remember to keep using this commitment every morning:

*"I make a decision never again to use violence against anyone, especially not against ------, and I will repeat this decision as often as is necessary to free my life completely from violent behaviour."*

**Case study 1:**

Lennox (not his real name) was born in the Caribbean but moved to England at a young age to be with his dad and stepmother. He came to the Everyman Centre in a very distressed state, he had punched his wife in her eyes and there was a possibility that she could lose her sight. He was inconsolable and wept for a while and I encouraged his tears. After he had finished crying I listened to his story and started to work immediately on raising his self-esteem, as he was very remorseful and in danger of harming himself.

After a few sessions I learnt from Lennox that his father had spent time in the military and had run the house like an army camp; everything had to be just right or else they were beaten. Lennox had been married a few years and began having problems with his partner when he tried to impose this same controlling behaviour on his wife. This led to many heated arguments that often ended with him "pummelling" her in the back with his fists. This struck me as being very strange behaviour and I pried to find out why that particular action.

After several sessions revisiting his childhood Lennox remembered that as a five-year-old he had seen his mother being bludgeoned to death. They had lived in a remote area and it was many hours before neighbours found him beside his mother's body.

We "worked" on this memory in several sessions as I took Lennox back to the scene time and time again. Each time he would cry and rage as hard as he could. After a while the memory did not have the same effect on him and he began to "make sense" of his behaviour.

After months of my working with Lennox his mood had improved as it became clear that his wife would not lose her sight. Lennox had generally been a very supportive husband. He loved his wife and wanted the best for her and worked hard to provide for them while she studied. They had several meetings over many weeks and she decided to give Lennox another chance. Many years after I had finished the sessions and his violence had completely stopped I was invited to the christening of their first child.

The case highlights a number of points:

- Feeling guilty about your violence will change nothing. What will stop your violence is action. You did not ask for the mistreatment and misinformation that made it possible for you to abuse someone but wallowing in self-pity will not change anything.

- Stopping the violence and working at rebuilding your self-esteem is important in overcoming the violent patterns. Try to remember that you are inherently good and reach for the memories of the times you were certain of your goodness.

- Separation ensured that the violence stopped while Lennox worked at building his self-esteem and received counselling to stop his violent behaviour.

- Controlling patterns of behaviour learnt in childhood from the adults around us influence the way we in turn behave as adults. The violence started when Lennox tried to impose the controlling behaviour he had learnt from his dad.

- It is possible to change. Lennox not only stopped his violence but also benefited from learning new ways of relating.

## Advocates

Taking a stand against domestic violence will help you to stop your violence. Many of the perpetrators I have worked with proudly recounted how they had made interventions since they started the group-work sessions. It does not sit comfortably with us to advocate against something and then engage in the very behaviour. To put an end to domestic violence requires everyone getting involved. No longer must the excuse be that it is a "personal" matter. As you begin to intervene others will learn from this and do the same. For example my sons, who are aware of my work with perpetrators, have told me of the times they interrupted violence to women in the streets and in clubs. What is encouraging is that their friends supported them when they intervened. I am pleased they have never used violence in their interventions. Imagine what it would be like if everyone who could intervene to stop domestic violence did so? Perpetrators would quickly get the message that their violence is unacceptable behaviour that will not be tolerated. A word of caution here, though: sometimes perpetrators are prepared to attack anyone who challenges their dominance of their partner. Make sure you have support if the situation looks more than you can handle. Intervention does not have to be physical; shouting "Stop it" from a safe distance can also make a difference.

## My story: Interrupting domestic violence

As mentioned earlier, I made a decision during one of my sessions always to interrupt domestic violence wherever I saw it occurring. Well, I had a busy six months doing just that and seriously wondered how it was all going to end. The first time was two weeks after making the decision; I was returning home one evening with a friend when I saw small crowd at the other side of the road. A woman was lying on the pavement with a man standing over her in an aggressive manner. I suspected what was happening and had my friend quickly stop the car. I got out, ran across the road, knelt beside the woman and enquired where she was hurt. I could see that she was really frightened, as she pleaded: "Please don't let him take me with him." The man meanwhile was busy having a row with the people who had gathered, but he soon turned his attention towards me. "Who the fuck are you? Doctor or something?"

I raised my hand, signalling "stop" to silence him as I tried to find out from the woman if she needed medical assistance. He continued his confrontation with the crowd. I could see no obvious injury but she was clearly very afraid to go with this man. I then stood up and as he faced me I said: "She is hurt and needs help and won't be going with you."

He went ballistic! Raising his voice even louder, he demanded: "Who the fuck do you think you are? Trying to take my woman?"

We were standing eyeball-to-eyeball. I only had to nod to deliver a head-butt. He was about my height and I had never lost a fight to anyone my size or weight so I was not about to be intimidated by this man, who had clearly been drinking too much. He eventually backed off when he understood that I was not afraid of him, nor was I going to budge an inch. Shortly after, the police arrived on the scene and he was arrested for possessing a dangerous weapon. I then learned from the crowd that they had tried to intervene but he had pulled a knife on them.

The mistaken assumption that domestic violence is a personal matter is widespread and must be challenged; it is unacceptable for anyone to beat up someone, partner or not. On another occasion I interrupted a man who was behaving very aggressively towards a woman who was trying to walk away from him. I crossed the road, heading directly towards him with "What's going on?" in an assertive but not aggressive tone. He stopped and as he started speaking to me the woman took the opportunity to walk away.

I could see he was very upset. I was pleasantly surprised that he thanked me for intervening and he soon calmed down as I listened to his story.

It was not all plain sailing. Another time a woman told me to "fuck off" at a busy train station when I responded to the sound of a slap coming from her direction. I could understand her hurt feelings and my putting attention on it that she did not want. The couple walked away and I held back — a bit embarrassed but at least I had offered to help. I soon realized that violence to women was a huge problem in this city. I would have my work cut out if I was going to keep to my commitment always to intervene.

I always avoided getting physical to stop the violence; only once did I have to, with one persistent abuser at a bus stop, who continued hitting his girlfriend as soon as my back was turned. It occurred to me that another way had to be found, as I was sure to get hurt or hurt someone if I kept interrupting violence in the streets or wherever. It is important that we not be silent spectators to domestic violence; but a word of caution here when trying to intervene. Always be aware that you can easily become the target of attack sometimes from both partners, as often the survivor is terrified of the attacker and feels obliged to show loyalty to them. There are many ways to intervene; shouting "stop it" from a safe distance is one I have mentioned, which I have used when I could not be sure where the abuse was happening.

### Healing the Hurts

**Session time:** To stop your violent behaviour you must heal from the hurts that were inflicted on you. You would not hurt anyone if you were not mistreated or seen mistreatment in the first place. Talking about and expressing feelings about the violence you have experienced helps to heal the wounds. Each one of us have our own unique experiences, every story is different. As I listen to you, my role is to help you notice where you were hurt and give you time to feel and express any feelings you may have. I will challenge any attempts to "minimize" the violence you perpetrated or that was done to you. This may take several sessions to cover and we will have to revisit some of the hurts you experienced until you are able to acknowledge and express some feelings about them. Being in denial about the hurts that were inflicted on you will hamper the recovery process. I need to hear about those early experiences from you.

I will do all I can to help you, but it really is down to you. Only you can stop your violence; there is no magic pill. You have to work consistently at this; I will put all of my experience, skill and love into helping you stop your violence, but I need you to work with me. I know we can work together to break the cycle of violence. Feeling bad about yourself will not help you change your behaviour. Taking action to make sure it never happens again is what is required of you. Wallowing in self-pity or looking for sympathy for your situation is not productive. The earlier you can move on from this phase the better.

Talking about your abuse will help you overcome it. Feelings may come up as you think about it; that is a good sign. Allow the feelings to show, it is a part of the healing process. I am sorry you hurt the one you love. It was wrong to abuse. It never must happen again; you have to make the decision never to abuse and keep making it every day, every time you think of the one you hurt make that decision.

**Exercise: Early memories.** What mistreatment did you experience as a child? Take time to have feelings about them.

Domestic violence is not inevitable; it is learned behaviour that can be unlearned. It has a beginning and must have an ending. Your actions can help bring about an end to domestic violence. By making a decision to take a stand against all forms of violence you will help to bring about the desired "zero tolerance" to domestic violence. Understanding how socialization for violence affects your behaviour is important in devising a plan to stop it. We will take a closer look at socialization for violence, especially as it affects men, in the next chapter. The "oppression of men" also deeply affects women, so I hope you too will stay engaged.

# CHAPTER TWO

.............................

## MEN'S LIBERATION

S ometimes when speaking about the liberation of men I have been met with anger and disbelief. It is hard for people to accept or imagine how, in our present patriarchal societies, organized mainly for the benefit of men, men could possibly be oppressed. After discussion, women do begin to understand that society can also disadvantage men. Black men, because of their experience of racism have little problem with the notion, but most white men find it hard to accept. This is not surprising, given the history of white conquest and domination of the world and its resources. Everywhere white men have gone they have conquered, raped, enslaved and often annihilated the indigenous population. White men have a history as oppressor, so it is hard for them to see that they too can be oppressed.

The confusion about men's oppression is understandable; with other oppressions there usually is an identifiable "other" group doing the oppressing. For example, with anti-Semitism it is gentiles doing the oppressing, with white racism it is white people oppressing black people. With the oppression of women, men are the oppressors. With the oppression of men there is no one group, but society as a whole does the oppressing, through its customs, culture and institutions. Chief among these latter are the army, police, prison and economic system.

Men do not like to think of themselves as victims; it does not square with what they have been socialized all their lives to believe of themselves. Men have been conditioned to believe they are superior to women. Since men control most of the economic, military and political power and have dominance over women, it is hard for them to see that they can be oppressor and also be oppressed at the same time. On closer scrutiny, it will be noticed that in fact it is a tiny minority of men who own and control most of the world's resources. The majority of men do not benefit hugely from the present oppressive system and many lose their lives prematurely because of it. Men, generally, feel better than women by belonging to this group and often are paid and valued more for the same work that women do, but these advantages are tiny compared to how their lives could be if there was no oppression.

Men need liberation because the majority of men live limited lives. The oppression forces men to behave badly and this is reflected in the violence men do to women and to other men. Too many men die needlessly in wars and at work. Men live shorter and unhealthier lives, and are more prone to alcohol and drug addiction. Men make up a huge worldwide prison population. Seventy-five per cent of suicides are by males and men are more likely to be institutionalized for mental health problems.

The suicide rate for young men is on a continual upward spiral, doubling since the early 1980s; in the same period it has halved for women. Men suffer all manner of stress-related illnesses yet 40 per cent of males visit the doctor only when their partners insist .[1] Men's lives are treated as dispensable and as being less deserving of care, especially in times of war, when they have been considered merely the "fuel" of the war machine. Men accept the notion that the lives of women and children are treated as more important. Men get to feel bad continually; every day the news is full of stories of violent crime, murder, rape and paedophilia committed by men, perpetuating a negative stereotype of men. Men may numb themselves from these bad feelings by indulging in risk taking, addictive behaviour and using mind-altering substances.

It is no fiction that men's lives are treated as less important; an official report reveals that the UK government spends eight times as much on women's health as it does on men's health.[2] Prostate cancer kills around 10,000 men a year; that is four times the number of women who die of cervical cancer over the same period, yet research into prostate cancer gets £37,000 a year as compared with £4.3 million a year spent on breast cancer research.[3]

Here are some of the grim statistics about men's health:

- The average life expectancy of a male born in the UK in 1997 is less than 75 years.
- Working-class men have a life expectancy of less than 70 years.
- The average man can expect to be seriously or chronically ill for 15 years of his life.
- The majority of men are too heavy for their health: 45 per cent are medically defined as overweight and the number of obese men is spiralling out of control, rising from 13.2 per cent in 1993 to 23.6 per cent in 2004.
- 28 per cent of men still smoke.
- 27 per cent of men drink alcohol at a level that could be harmful for their health.
- 41 per cent of male deaths under the age of 75 are caused by circulatory diseases, the largest single cause of death. Each year over 130,000 men of all ages die from these diseases.

- Of these deaths, over two-thirds are due to coronary heart disease.
- Prostate cancer is the most common cancer affecting men alone. Nearly 22,000 men in the UK are newly diagnosed with prostate cancer each year and about 9,500 die annually. The number of new cases is expected to treble over the next 20 years.
- The suicide rate among men is increasing, with the rate doubling for men aged between 15 and 24 in the past 25 years.
- Many men are affected by sexual problems. Recent research in the USA suggest that almost a third of men of all ages say they climax too early and nearly a fifth of men in their fifties experience problems achieving or maintaining an erection.[4]

The authors of the above statistics on men's health believe they are so bad because men are still brought up to believe that they must be strong and tough, and behave as if they are indestructible. This makes it hard for them to look after their health or seek a doctor's help.

On average, British men die some six years younger than women and there is a difference in life expectancy, depending on class and location. Women in the richer south of the UK live up to 13.8 years longer than men in the poorer north, while men in richer southern areas live up to ten years longer than men in the poorer north. Manchester had the lowest life expectancy for men at 69.7 years of age compared with 79.6 in north Dorset, the UK's highest rate. Men have closed the gap in Dorset to three and a half years with women,[5] but this still leaves room for improvement, as a study of 222 prehistoric skeletons showed that the average life span for Neolithic adult males was 34.3 years, for females it was 29.8 years.[6]

Poverty is a significant factor in determining life expectancy but other factors also contribute to men's early death; more men than women smoke, drink, take risks with their lives and work longer hours in harsh conditions.

A recent survey found that a "third of men were drinking to drown out stress", 40 per cent of them had difficulty switching off from work, with 22 per cent suffering from job-related stress, 20 per cent had "aggressive outbursts", 15 per cent had lower sex drives and 5 per cent suffered sexual impotence.[7]

**Exercise for men and women: Healthy living.** Take time to think/ talk about what aspects of your health you have neglected. What do you need to change and what support do you need to make those changes? How will you get the support you need?

The oppression of men begins at an early age with the almost universal "big boys don't cry". This early interruption of one of the natural healing processes of the body leaves men with a great deal of unhealed hurt, which has an adverse effect on their lives. "Boys are conditioned to repress feelings of weakness, fear, or vulnerability. As a consequence, their emotional repertoire is much more limited than that of girls and so is their ability to empathize."[8] Crying is important for our wellbeing. Notice how when young ones get hurt in any way they cry naturally if allowed to; after a good cry, they soon revert to their delightful happy selves, especially if given a sympathetic hug and some attention. Girls are generally given a little more space to cry but boys are often quickly, systematically excluded from this process and as a result store up many more unhealed hurts. To stop boys from showing feelings, then later on in life blame them for not "having any feelings", is oppressive.

The oppression of men has gone on for so long and has been internalized so completely men believe that it is "natural". They have accepted as theirs the stereotype of being providers and protectors. In prehistoric times when men had to fight for scarce resources they learnt to mistrust other men.

During the formation of archaic states, men were coerced into fighting and made to feel proud to die for "king and country". Skill at fighting marked men out for distinction; one of the greatest honours bestowed on a British and Commonwealth citizen is the Victoria Cross for valour "in the face of the enemy". Men cannot end oppression if they do not see it. The oppression of men is rooted in class oppression and began with the accumulation of land and wealth and the acquisition of slaves. The "survival of the fittest" philosophy, nurtured for centuries, has been used as an excuse to keep men fighting and to justify exploiting the weak. The widespread belief that men must fight for survival has served to reinforce male oppression, but not all agree with the notion. Let us look at some of the arguments.

## Nature versus Nurture

The argument about whether men are aggressive by nature or nurture has been raging for centuries. It has recently been ignited in a book which argues that men rape because they are programmed to do so: "We fervently believe that just as the leopard's spots and the giraffe's elongated neck are the results of eons of past Darwinian selection, so also is rape."[9] For the rapist, this is a welcome excuse for their predatory behaviour; for those who think little of men, it is confirmation for them that men are inherently flawed; maybe it might just be true that men are from Mars. This kind of thinking is an excuse for men to not take responsibility for their actions and it ignores some of the real causes of rape. If it is true that rapists have no control over their behaviour, what is the point of trying to change something that has been determined long before they were born? Having worked with rapists in a prison and seeing the level of denial about their crime, it worries me that this kind of propaganda will only encourage the rapists and make it much more difficult for them to accept responsibility.

Two other authors, Oliver James and Steven Pinker, had a slanging match over the roots of violence. James in his book *"They F\*\*\* You Up"* argues that family influences are critical and that children's violent behaviour is picked up from parents. Pinker in *The Blank Slate* argues that violent roots are deep and innate and that violent tendencies are inherited.[10] No doubt the "nature v. nurture" debate will continue until there is conclusive evidence on either side to call a halt.

Some of the difficulty with proving the arguments about "nature or nurture" is that the research and experiments to explain and understand human behaviour is often carried out on animals. For example, an experiment by Zing Yang Kuo attempted to explode the myth that cats will instinctively stalk rats. He raised a kitten and a rat in the same cage and they became companions and, what's more, the *cat refused to chase or kill* other rats.[11] On the other hand another experiment showed that a rat raised in isolation will attack a fellow rat if introduced to the cage, showing that aggression does not need to be learned.[12] Although the experiment by Zing Yang Kuo does not prove that cats do not instinctively kill rats, it proves that aggressive behaviour can be inhibited by early experience.

From a survey of the evidence on aggression, it was concluded that there is "no inborn need for fighting". If an organism can organize its life so there is no outside stimulation to fight, then it will not experience any psychological or mental damage as a result of not expressing aggression.[13] This view contradicts Freud's contention and, in effect, asserts there is no instinct of aggression. One of the leading experts on human aggression, Leonard Berkowitz, believes humans are essentially different from non-humans in that learning plays a more important role in aggressive behaviour. There is ample evidence to support his contention that "among humans, innate patterns of behaviour are infinitely modifiable and flexible".[14] For example the primitive Tasaday tribe, only recently "discovered" in a remote area of the Philippine Islands, live in cooperative friendliness, both within their own tribe, and in their relations with others. Similar observations were made among the Lepchas of Sikkim, the Pygmies of Central Africa, and the Arapesh of New Guinea. Acts of aggression are extremely rare and they have no word for war.[15]

Also changing social conditions within a given culture can lead to changes in aggressive behaviour. For example, the Iroquois Indians lived in peace for hundreds of years as a hunting nation until in the seventeenth century a growing trade with the newly arrived Europeans brought the Iroquois into direct competition with the neighbouring Hurons over furs (to trade for manufactured goods). A series of wars developed and the Iroquois became ferocious and successful warriors, not because of uncontrollable aggressive instincts, but because a social change created a situation that increased competition.[16]

The stereotyping of men as naturally violent has been carefully nurtured by a system with an interest in having men fight wars. One of the earliest, enduring violent images is the cartoon depiction of "caveman", club in hand, dragging cave woman by her hair. This false representation of Neanderthals, despite evidence of his "essential gentleness",[17] has left many of us with the belief that men have always been violent to women. Just as we have been led to believe that competition and aggression are necessary for our survival, we have been lied to about the true nature of men. Men's violent behaviour has more to do with socialization than anything else. *In Boys will be Boys* Myriam Miedzian shows how Harvard professor Edward O. Wilson argued that "while human behaviour is based on biology and its origin can be traced through evolutionary theory of adaptation, it can only be fully understood through the interaction of biology and culture, and the weight of culture is enormous."[18] Let us take a look at how the socialization for violence affects us as individuals.

## My story: Socialization for violence

I grew up in a rough village where the socialization for violence was relentless. My role models were the "hard" men of the village. My toys were guns, knives, swords, arrows and bow, which we mostly made ourselves. I was often hit by my parents and had regular fights with my siblings. We loved Westerns and violent martial arts movies. We fought a lot in school and on the streets. I sometimes even left the classroom to have a fight, but most fighting was done at break times. Sometimes teachers did their best to stop us fighting and when it became more difficult to have a fight at school, we arranged fights after school, away from the teacher's gaze.

When James (not his real name) joined our school, he came with a reputation and the other students wanted to see us fight. He looked tough and I definitely was not looking for a fight with him. Maybe he made the same assessment of me, for we never fought but became friends. James and I used to practise head-butts after school, standing toe to toe, butting each other on the forehead. After we finished secondary school James went on to build a reputation as one of the "baddest" men in the country.

Saturday night entertainment in the village was a juke-box on the street corner with vendors selling food and drink. Usually there was at least one fight on the night between the older boys or men, which sometimes got quite nasty and involved bottles, knives, cutlasses or paling staves; but mostly it was clean fist fights, since to resort to using weapons was almost an admission of weakness during this period.

I had my share of fights in the village but I moved to a mining town after leaving secondary school when I was accepted for an apprenticeship in the bauxite industry. I had a few arguments here with other boys but nothing serious, until one confrontation with John, whom I had allowed to move into my flat, after two weeks of his constant pestering. One day while he was at work my girlfriend Fauzia used a couple of his cigarettes. When he returned later he became irate with me for taking his cigarettes without permission. The fuss he made in front of Fauzia really embarrassed me. I could understand his annoyance but he carried on to such an extent that I angrily told him to leave. John packed his things and left in a rage.

It was a few months after this incident that John found an opportunity to pick a fight with me. I was sitting on a settee, glass in hand at a party, when John approached me rudely. "Move - I want to lie down," he said, as he moved to sit at the other end of the settee. I simply ignored this affront. He swivelled on his seat, lifting and swinging his legs, which were about to land in my lap. I caught his left leg with one hand and flung it away from my body, causing him to fall from the chair. He was quickly on his feet and reaching into his pocket with his right hand. I could see the knife being pulled. I grabbed his knife-hand with my left hand, at the same time breaking my glass on the floor. The glass broke badly, leaving me with the near-useless base, which I pressed into John's wrist, cutting him slightly. We were swiftly separated and John was escorted down the steps. From the front yard he challenged me to "come down and fight." I said nothing, but stood on the balcony, glaring at him.

Well, I had never backed down from a fight, but I was not suicidal. Here was a guy bigger in size and age, armed with a knife, and me with nothing to defend myself. I ignored the challenge and his final threat before leaving was: "Any time I see you I'm going to chop you up." I had a few more drinks then headed for home as darkness set in, aware that I could be attacked from any number of blind spots on the route home.

This bothered me; I had never walked the streets in fear before and I was not about to start now. I was worried about where all this would lead, though, and thought of going to the police station. The police probably would take no action anyway and word would soon spread that I was seeking police protection. I ruled this out, as I reckoned it would give John a psychological advantage if he thought I was afraid of him.

Now, I was taking John dead seriously so next day I made a dagger, twice the length of the six-inch blade he had pulled on me. I was not going to wait to be attacked. That was never my style; I almost always got the first blow in, if I felt a fight was inevitable. I needed to settle this fight quickly, for I enjoyed a drink and was always walking late and often alone at night.

A week after the threat I armed myself and went looking for John. I decided first to visit my grandmother who was in hospital, as it might be a long time before I had the opportunity again, if ever. Sitting in her room overlooking the entrance to the hospital grounds, I saw John and a friend approaching the hospital gate. I quickly said my goodbyes and left the room thinking about the best spot for this impending fight. I decided on the open space used as the reception area at the entrance of the hospital; at least medical treatment would not be far away and I had lots of room for manoeuvring.

Now, the hospital compound was a popular meeting place for young people on a Sunday afternoon, as we dressed up to go visiting friends or family, or to just hang out to meet the opposite sex. My girlfriend Fauzia was at the hospital and I told her what was going on, that I had seen John approaching the hospital with his friend, who was at least six feet two inches tall; I knew him well enough to know that he did not like me.

The adrenalin was pumping. I was tense but focused on the fight and what I had to do. I had no doubt that I was fighting for my manhood; I would rather die than not walk tall and proud anywhere, anytime. I had prepared myself mentally: I might get injured, but that would not prevent me being the victor. Fauzia said she would get between us to stop the fight. I warned her not to as any such attempt by her would make the situation dangerous for us both.

I was actually encouraged by the sight of John approaching with his friend. He couldn't be that fearless then, I reasoned. The bad men in the village where I grew up were loners; they never ganged up on anyone. I also felt I had the right to use any means necessary to protect myself if ganged up on.

I had learnt the hard way never to reach for a weapon unless I was prepared to use it from a fight with one of my brothers. During one of our many fights I had picked up a plank of wood with the intention of warding him off; he also grabbed a length of wood but immediately delivered a blow to my hand. I was reeling in pain and nursing a swollen wrist for days but I had learnt my lesson.

John entered the waiting area, saw Fauzia and me and came straight for us. I was leaning against the handrail used as a partition for patients queuing to collect their prescriptions. He stopped about six feet away and pulled out his pocket-knife, opening it almost casually. "Let's finish it now," he said. I don't know what he was expecting. He seemed so casual and self-assured! Maybe he thought I would run, apologize, beg, or something. I could not believe his arrogance. I had my ten-inch dagger concealed in a newspaper, which I had folded into a sheath for the blade. I had pinned it with my left forearm to the handrail, against which I was leaning, with the handle in easy reach of my right hand but concealed from John.

Well, I was not wasting my breath. I quickly drew my dagger, took one stride with my left foot towards John and plunged the dagger straight at his chest. I was surprised. I could not believe I was so close and had missed him! He had reacted defensively much faster than I expected. His feet were firmly planted on the ground, slightly apart, and by bending his knees forward and rocking his body back, at an almost impossible angle, avoided my thrust. The adrenalin was pumping. This was life-or-death stuff, no time for missing – it could cost me my life. I shuffled my feet to recover my balance, this time dropping my right shoulder lower to the ground, making myself a smaller target and preparing for an upward thrust to his gut.

A good move, except that there was no one there to stab. John had wheeled on his heel in an about-turn and was off in a flash. Not before I had seen the white of his eyes, though; they had popped as though about to fall out. I gave chase, but this guy was fast, I never knew he could run like that. I gave up the chase after about fifty yards. I then retreated and started to panic a bit. Where was his friend? He had disappeared. Maybe they were going to regroup and come at me again. I ran over to cover the likely route they could use to get back at me. My brain was racing with the adrenalin pumping and I could not bring myself to a stop. Fauzia grabbed hold of me and held on. I slowed down, and my body started shaking uncontrollably as the realization that I could have killed John sank in; or maybe it was relief that I was not going to prison after all, that I had seen off the attack without getting hurt or drawing blood. My worst fear was having my gut ripped as I had seen done to someone in my village.

I had seen the fear in John's eyes and was no longer afraid of him. I could "take" him anytime. I have never stabbed anyone and was relieved to no longer feel that I had to arm myself. I left my dagger at home the very next day I was out walking with a friend. Sure enough, there was John and his friends. Word travels fast here and I knew they would have heard of the fight. I was heading straight for them. Well, I couldn't avoid them; they were on the pavement of the main road I was walking. I quickly changed my step, from a casual one to a more deliberate step, with a sense of purpose. Walking with my left hand clasped firmly to my side as though concealing a weapon, right hand swinging, ready for swift action. They would have understood that I was signalling I had a concealed weapon in my waist.

This was risky, but I was on a high, ready to fight, armed or not, and I held the memory of his eyes "popping" firmly in my mind. They were watching my approach and as I got close enough to John, with a deliberate, quick motion I swung my right arm across my body as though reaching for a weapon. I was taking a calculated risk, going against the lesson learnt from my brother, but I trusted my judgement. John leapt across a huge drain into the road to avoid me. I stopped and pressed home my advantage to the maximum. "Don't jump! Don't fuck with me or I will kill you!" I stood and stared at him for a short while. He backed off to a safe distance, keeping his eyes on me as I walked away.

Next evening I was out John came over to me with a half-apology. "Let's forget the story," he said. I looked him in the eye and replied, "Don't want one. But don't fuck with me." Never had any more trouble from John, and he was always quick to greet me whenever he saw me. Last time I saw him, many years after the incident, we talked and joked for a while, and he was helpful to me as a money changer.

> **Exercise: Noticing the socialization.** What was the socialization for violence like for you? Take time to pay attention to any feelings that may come up as you talk/think or write about your experience.

### Internalized men's oppression

When men think and behave in the manner of the stereotypes created for them, they have "internalized" the oppression. Many men feel responsible for providing and protecting their families and if they are unable to do so they feel like failures. At the extreme end this disappointment can lead to some men taking their lives; as men they find it hard to ask for help. Some groups such as farmers, police and doctors are especially vulnerable to suicide, because asking for help is seen as a weakness. Patriarchal rule has left men with a skewed picture of masculinity and many feel confused about what is expected of them in relationships. They may internalize the violent male stereotype and act it out on other men and women.

## Providers

Boys have the expectation put on them very early on in life that someday they will have to provide for a family. They will be given toys that help prepare them for their working life, be it doctor, carpenter, scientist, mechanic, soldier, etc. The myth of "man the hunter" served to propagate the notion of male hegemony and was useful for the owners of the means of production in their exploitation of the working class. Men were socialized to see themselves as the providers and during the industrial revolution women were expected to stay at home to service the men whose role it was to "bring home the bacon". Lerner argues that the myth of man the hunter came late in the development of society and anyway the same conditions do not exist today to justify a division of labour.[19]

Despite more women having an active economic role, the stereotyping of men as providers remains a dominant one, causing men to feel responsible for providing and feeling bad if they don't. A study by the Samaritans in the 1980s in an area of Glasgow with high rates of suicides by young men showed that unemployment was a factor in their deaths. There are hopeful signs that these attitudes are beginning to shift in some places as a recent study showed that some 82 per cent of girls and 64 per cent of boys disagreed that "a man's job is to earn the money: a woman's job to look after the home and family".[20]

## Killers

In prehistoric times men often had to fight for land and resources for their survival, so it may be true that the societies that survived and prospered were the ones that were good at fighting. The use of violence was widespread in the establishment and maintenance of most nation states. As a result, violent patterns of behaviour, passed on from one generation to the next, are now deeply ingrained in most societies today. The socialization for violence is what makes war possible; there would be no wars if men refused to fight. The states' dependence on men being prepared to fight is one reason why the socialization for violence is one of the most important factors in the oppression of men. While it may be the case that in the past our survival depended on men's fighting skills, this is no longer true of modern man; yet the socialization for violence continues relentlessly with increased sophistication.

In times of war men often find themselves in a position of "kill or be killed", if not by the enemy then by their own army. Most fighting nations have in the past executed their own soldiers in battle, with some 306 British soldiers executed in World War 1 for cowardice, quitting their post or desertion. Many were teenagers at the time they joined the army.

The socialization for violence begins from the time boys are put in blue and handled less or more roughly as babies.[21] Before they can walk they have often been given an arsenal of war toys. They will soon have an Action Man, Spiderman or one of the Super Heroes to play with. Boys have the expectation put on them to be tough and strong and if they don't conform to this stereotype they will be called "sissy", or other derogatory names and will be beaten, if they refuse to fight. The violent stereotyping of men is responsible for much of the pain men feel and perpetrate in the world today, it has left men being mistrustful of each other and prevents them making friends easily. Men cannot look at each other for any length of time without it being seen as a challenge. One perpetrator I worked with recounted how he was about to get off a bus, when he looked at a man and they ended up "staring each other down". He missed his stop rather than be the first to look away. Recently a man aged 43 was murdered after a "staring out" confrontation with four youths.[22] The conditioning is so pervasive it is a wonder that most men are able to reject this violent stereotyping.

## Men and War

War dehumanizes us all; even if we do not participate in it directly we are affected by its consequences. Most of us switch off or just numb out on war reporting. This is not surprising as violence is thrown at us on a daily basis that we can only take so much. No other institution bears more responsibility for men's oppression than the military. Wars have taken a large proportion of men's lives throughout the short history of the world, with millions and millions of men killed and millions more maimed and traumatized for life.

In the First World War alone, those killed comprised 1.8 million Germans, 1.7 million Russians, 1.4 million French, 1.2 million Austro-Hungarians, 900,000 from Britain and her empire, 650,000 Italians, hundreds of thousands of other nationalities, and treble these numbers of wounded, many of whom never fully recovered. Civilian deaths were estimated at 7 million, the total number of deaths about 15 million.[23] World War 2 saw even more carnage, with some 60 countries involved, and "cost 55 million dead, including 27 million Russians and 6 million Jews... it set new standards for barbarity in the heartlands of the European enlightenment."[24] As J. K Galbraith put it, "The roll-call of dead and maimed and mentally annihilated is staggering." He adds: "Wars are a major threat to civilized existence, and a corporate commitment to weapons procurement and use nurtures this threat. It accords legitimacy and even heroic virtue, to devastation and death." [25]

**Session time:** Some of you may have been involved in the military or have had someone close to you involved. Some of the reading here will seem harsh on the military establishment, but I have felt it necessary to put the case against war strongly as it is the single most important factor in the overall socialization for violence for men. If you have military experience you may find yourself becoming defensive. You must resist this; it is not a criticism of you but of the system that pressures men into this situation. There may be things you have seen or done that you need to recover from. The pressure for you to not acknowledge your pain is part of the male conditioning that you must overcome to seek help. It is useful to keep remembering that you are inherently good, no matter what has happened to dehumanize you, and that you can recover your full humanity, with a bit of support. There are some organizations that support veterans and you may need to seek help if you feel affected by involvement in military action.

> **Exercise: The effects of war.** If you have received military training or seen active duty talk/think or write about how it has affected you. If you have not been in the military, do you know anyone who has seen active duty and how do you think it has affected their behaviour?

### Domestic Violence and War

Research has shown that in times of war domestic violence increases in the countries involved.[26] One study compared the crime rates of roughly 110 countries since 1900; they found that war actually encourages domestic violence. Only recently it was reported how, during one six-week spell, four US army soldiers killed their wives after returning from active duty in Afghanistan. The chairwoman of the Defence Department's Task Force on Domestic Violence is reported to have said: "This does really feel unusual to have so many partners killed in such a short time in one place." All the soldiers had been stationed at Fort Bragg, three of them members of the Special Forces.

Congress established the Defence Department Task Force in 1999 after finding that the incidence of domestic violence in the military had risen to 25.6 per 1,000 soldiers in 1996 from 18.6 per 1,000 in 1990, while domestic violence rates were declining in the overall populace. Ms Hansen of the Miles Foundation (an advocacy group for victims of military domestic violence) said: "A series of studies had shown that the rate of domestic violence in the military was two to five times higher than in the civilian population." She added: "The numbers have been sharply debated by experts and are difficult to calculate because the military only counts married couples in incidents of domestic violence, not former spouses or girlfriends."[27]

## Mistreatment of men

It is ironic that patriarchal societies, set up for male privilege, can be so uncaring to the majority of men. Nothing is spared in preparing men to kill (and even that is in doubt after recent events in Iraq, about lack of equipment) but when it comes to taking care of them after risking life and limb, support is woefully lacking as lance-corporal Johnson Beharry, who was awarded the Victoria Cross found out. He complained about the lack of treatment that he and troops returning from Iraq and Afghanistan received for suffering from "combat stress, depression and mental trauma". The Ministry of Defence responded by saying they provided the "'very best" diagnosis and treatment.[28]

Falklands war veterans claim that a lack of resources to tackle post-traumatic stress disorder has meant that suicide has claimed more lives than were actually lost in the conflict. Chris Duggan, who received a Mental Health Media Award for speaking out about his condition, said: "There were 256 British fatalities in the Falklands, but there have been well over 300 suicides since. There was one three weeks ago. You hear of so many taking to drugs or alcohol." One veteran, Charles Bruce, jumped 5,000 feet from a plane without a parachute. He had previously tried to drown himself in a bathtub and had also failed to burn himself.[29] Still not enough is known about the illnesses affecting veterans and many conditions remain untreated after involvement in war - this despite some 80,000 veterans deemed to have suffered shell shock in the Great War almost 100 years ago.

Men experience all kinds of horrific conditions in wartime and need support to get over those experiences or they may be traumatized for the rest of their lives. Many suffer from nightmares and uncontrollable flashbacks of wartime incidents some 50 years after they had happened. According to a survey of Second World War veterans one in five suffer from "mental and emotional distress as a result of combat experience,"[30] Duggan believes there are no easy solutions. "You can teach a man to kill, but you can't teach a man to die or see death and dying," he says. "Nothing can prepare you for that...." He found the government's response to the soldiers' difficulties woefully lacking, amounting to: "That's it, Tommy Atkins. Give us your rifle back and you can fuck off."[31] He may have a point as many are sleeping rough and 9 per cent of former soldiers end up in a prison cell, because of excess alcohol or drug taking leading to violent offences according to a recent report.[32] Some who do not end up in prison end up committing suicide according to research funded by the MoD veterans aged under 24 were at particular risk "They were two to three times more likely to kill themselves than civilian men of the same age."

One 80-year-old veteran of the First World War killed his neighbour after being woken by fireworks and suffering a flashback. "I heard gunfire," he told police. "I thought I was back. I must have heard the noise outside and I must have picked up a knife and gone outside. I saw a dim figure in front of me and I was sure he was a German. I stabbed twice." When he came to himself he realized he had stabbed his 85-year-old neighbour. He told the police: "I'm sorry I done it. I'm not going to deny it." Later he explained to detectives: "I thought I was back in the war. I done the murder. What else is there to say?" Asked why he had stabbed her twice, he said: "I don't know. Just what you always used to do, wasn't it? To make sure." The defendant spent five months in prison before being sectioned under the Mental Health Act, permitting him to be detained in hospital pending the preparation of reports.[33]

It is not only in the theatre of war that men are not given due consideration as complaints about the sub-standard housing conditions for them and their family, have come to light in the press. Past and present generals have complained about lack of equipment, training and pay. "Military operations cost in blood and treasure, because risk free soldiering, which some seem to think is possible, is simply a contradiction in terms. "It is our soldiers who pay the cost in blood; the nation must therefore pay the cost in treasure. Soldiers and their families must be properly valued." Only after a number of embarrassing headlines have the government taken steps to rectify the situation by offering a new deal for the armed forces and their families ranging from better accommodation, big increases in compensation for badly wounded soldiers, priority for medical treatment and free education for veterans. [34]

Combat Stress is one group that helps soldiers; it treats annually some 2,000 veterans, aged from 19 to 96, who have survived the wars. John, who was 19 when he was sent to the Falklands, gets help; he shot an unarmed soldier his age and has not recovered from the experience after twenty years. "I never thought I would go to war," he says, "it was very inhuman, very alien. War is not a glorious thing and anyone who makes out it is is a fool."[35]

War is not only damaging and potentially deadly to the soldiers who participate in it but it also has an adverse effect on the population. Far more civilians than soldiers are killed and disabled in times of war and the proportion is climbing as more and more wars are fought, not on battlefields but in people's front yards. The proportion of civilian to military casualties has increased from 5 per cent in the First World War to 50 per cent in the Second and 90 per cent in more recent conflicts. Let us take a closer look at this so-called "collateral damage" of wars.

### Children and War

Far more children than soldiers are killed and disabled in times of war and the proportion keeps climbing. The danger for children not only lies with direct participation in wars but that they are most likely to be injured by antipersonnel mines and bomb lets, left after the war. The Red Cross has called for a ban on cluster bombs because "their indiscriminate nature means civilians are often the victims". Even the USA delivered "a mild but rare rebuke to Israel" after it dropped 100,000 cluster bombs in its attack on Lebanon.[36] The USA, Russia and the UK have long resisted a complete ban, but a new treaty has given campaigners against its use hope that some day they will no longer be used. The treaty signed by over 100 states including the UK gave campaigners hope that they will eventually force the USA, China, Russia, Israel, India, and Pakistan who were missing from the talks in Dublin to stop using these weapons.[37]

After ten years of sanctions on Iraq by the West, infant deaths soared by 600 per cent over the four years from 1990 to 1994 according to a WHO Report. Madeleine Albright, the then US Secretary of State, was asked: "We have heard that half a million children have died. I mean that's more children than died in Hiroshima. And - and, you know, is the price worth it?" She replied: "I think this is a very hard choice, but the price - I think the price is worth it."[38] For every child killed many more will be disfigured and scarred for life. They make up the figures for "collateral damage"; literally millions of children through no fault of theirs have paid the ultimate price. Relatively recently in the Gaza Strip it was reported that over 400 children were killed by the Israeli army in a very short period of occupation.

Children are not only indirectly affected by fighting; some are daily being coerced into fighting. A report from the Coalition to Stop the Use of Child Soldiers was highly critical of Britain "within Europe the UK has the lowest minimum age for recruitment, the highest recruitment of under-18s into the regular armed forces and the lowest deployment age. The UK is also the only European country to send minors routinely into battle."[39] The Ministry of Defence was "accused of supplying 'misleading propaganda' to schools and attempting to recruit pupils into the army" in Iraq. They were also accused by the Joseph Rowntree Charitable Trust of setting up websites "targeted at 12- to 17-year-olds, but noted that some recruitment tactics targeted children as young as seven." [40]

There are some positive developments: there are fewer conflicts in which children are involved, down from 27 in 2004 to 17 by the end of 2007. On the down side, a few British under-18s were deployed to Iraq up to 2005 and at least 63 governments, including the UK and the USA, still allow voluntary recruitment of under-18s despite the age of adulthood being set at 18.[41] Targeting the young seems set to continue, however, with prime minister Gordon Brown agreeing with "Controversial plans for pupils in comprehensive schools to sign up for military drills and weapons training" being proposed by a former Conservative minister who defected to the Labour Party.[42] This is an indication of how desperate they are for recruits, as it was reported that more people are leaving than joining the army with recruiters "concerned about the mum factor - mothers not wanting sons to be put in the line of fire and sent to Iraq."[43]

**Women and War**

Women have always suffered disproportionately in times of war, apart from the loss of sons, fathers, brothers, husbands, uncles, cousins and friends; women have historically been the spoils of war. Soldiers have always raped women from the defeated enemy as part of the prize of vanquisher and *Time Magazine* lamented in 1945 that it "has remained a feature of warfare and conquest from the second millennium B.C. to the present," adding: "Our own army and the British army along with ours have done their share of looting and raping...we too are considered an army of rapists"[44] All countries are implicated in this crime and we must not forget the 200,000 "comfort women" enslaved by the Japanese forces during the Second World War and who are still fighting for an apology and compensation.

In the Kosovan war, up to 20,000 Albanian women were raped by the Yugoslav police, the military, Serb paramilitaries and civilians, in their push to ethnically cleanse Kosovo of Albanians. It was reported that villages were searched for Albanian girls of child-bearing age to rape. Ahemeti, from the Centre for Protection of Women and Children was quoted:

"these are simple women, women who have been degraded, disgraced and will carry this trauma like a bullet, for the rest of their lives. Our society is a traditional one, where Albanian men are brought up to see themselves as breadwinners and protectors." She continues: "Once you touch the woman, you touch the honour of the family and you provoke the man to react...so daughters were gang raped in front of their fathers, wives in front of their husbands, nieces in front of their uncles, mothers in front of their children, just to dehumanise, just to degrade."[45] Still rape was only recognized as a crime against humanity in 2001 with a landmark judgment in The Hague that Amnesty International described as a "a significant step for women's human rights. Sexual enslavement in armed conflict is now legally acknowledged as a crime against humanity and perpetrators can and must be held to account".[46]

> **Exercise: Healing the hurts.** Take time to absorb the above and allow some feelings, make a decision to stop if you are engaged in violating women in any way and seek professional help to stop.

War corrupts everyone involved with this dirty work of humans killing humans. Let us look at what it does to the people and institutions that are deeply involved in the business of death and destruction.

## Governments

In Britain, when the Labour Party won the 1997 general election a new era was proclaimed. There was to be a government of openness, armed with an "ethical foreign policy", especially where arms sales were concerned. No longer would dictators be able to use British weapons against a civilian population, they promised. Unfortunately for the oppressed, these promises were broken even before the ink had time to dry.

All governments collude in the murky business of war that benefits the so-called defence industries handsomely. The British Tory government was accused of having "an unhealthily cosy relationship with a small coterie of the country's biggest defence contractors. This is taxpayers' money we are talking about. And the taxpayer has a right to know exactly how it is being spent."[47] The incoming Labour government's support for British defence companies also came under scrutiny with a report estimating that taxpayers spend £420m each year subsidizing the export of arms, although the Ministry of Defence strongly rejected the report's findings.

The relationship that the defence industry enjoys with government was brought into sharp focus when it stopped the Serious Fraud Office from pursuing a two-year investigation of the global defence company British Aerospace (BAE) and Saudi Arabian alleged corruption. As the Serious Fraud Office closed the net and were about to get access to telling bank accounts the Saudis threatened to pull the plug on the contracts and to stop cooperation with the intelligence services. They demanded an end to the investigations, giving a ten-day deadline. The government of the day responded by speedily dropping the case, with Prime Minister Tony Blair taking "full responsibility" for ending the enquiry. Sir Menzies Campbell, then Liberal Party leader, called it a "sorry day for Britain's reputation". Sir Nicholas Lyall, a former attorney-general, said that while he agreed with the judgment it was "absolutely astonishing" that Mr Blair should get involved in a matter for the independent prosecuting authority. The Conservative Party also challenge the government over other alleged corrupt deals made by BAE in Africa but "remain silent on allegations about the £43bn Saudi deal, originally drawn up by Mrs Thatcher in 1985". It is a murky trade indeed, with the Labour Party, local councils, charities and dozens of educational institutions having huge sums invested in British companies making huge profits from the arms trade. It was revealed that even "MP's retirement money had been invested in cigarette firms and arms manufacturers."[48]

Men have fought wars for a long, long time, and left to the war industry men will forever be at war. Men have progressed from fighting with bare hands to using clubs, spears, rocks and knives to guns. We have moved from war on land to war at sea and in the air. Some would see us fighting in space if they have their way. The makers of the tools of death and destruction have no concern for human suffering and invent some of the most horrific weapons that cause death in the most horrible and painful ways. Not only do bereaved families suffer loss and trauma, but for the veterans themselves a study found that "Many are still suffering nightmares and uncontrollable flashbacks of wartime incidents"[49]

## Change

Ways must be found to end conflicts, without the death and destruction to which we have grown so accustomed. It is imperative because "conflicts in our time can cause both a human and an environmental catastrophe".[50] Not only is there damage to the environment but also to the soldier's ability to produce healthy babies, as a result of exposure to harmful chemicals of the war industry. Then there is the financial cost of wars, the "largest spending in the world at over one trillion dollars in annual expenditure and has been rising in recent years."[51] Apart from the waste of taxpayers' money, how long are we prepared to keep sacrificing innocent lives? Are men destined perpetually to fight wars? Are our sons and their sons and daughters destined to pay the "blood price", and for how much longer? This spending is futile: there can be no "war to end all wars", for it is well established that violence breeds only more violence.

## Boxing

This so-called sport is second only to the military in responsibility for the violent stereotyping of men. This is the only sport in the world where the object is to cause pain or hurt someone, to the point of unconsciousness. As Mike Tyson put it: "You ask any boxer, whether he is Mohammed Ali or me, we're in the hurt business, I got no illusions about boxing — none. This is a brutal business. But I'm a fighter — that's all I can do. It's my destiny."[52]

Prior to the release of a film on Mohammed Ali's life, several programmes about him were shown on TV. I felt compelled to watch; he is such a beautiful, interesting, intelligent and skilful boxer. His face is recognized worldwide and we all love him. He took on the world and beat it several times over. He took on the US government over Vietnam and we cheered him. He stands for dignity, pride, strength and love for all black people and he is adored by all.

As I watched a documentary I was reminded of the research done after the much-publicized Ali v. Foreman "Rumble in the Jungle" fight. Sociologist David Phillips and his colleagues conducted extensive research on the impact of media violence on self-destructive behaviour such as suicides and aggressive behaviour such as homicides. The study found that in the days after a much-publicized prize fight more men died in the streets. They also found that there was a co-relation to race. If a white man was beaten more white men died in the streets next day. If a black man was beaten more black men died.[53] For decades now heavyweight fights have been about black men; one can only imagine what heavyweight fighting does for black on black violence. I have noted that Tupac, the famed rap singer, died the night of a Tyson fight. On the night of the much-hyped 1992 British heavyweight fight between Frank Bruno and Jose Ribalta, a black man was killed in London. Shortly after the fight Lloyd Anthony Davis, aged 28, was shot dead at point-blank range outside a pub. His friend, who was with him at the time of the shooting, said that a disagreement over the outcome of the fight led to an argument with Lloyd being racially abused before he was shot.[54]

The day before the fight the headlines in bold print were: "I don't care if I blind Bruno"; the Cuban boxer had argued that if Bruno knew he had a torn retina he should not fight and that he would make the eye a target. He added, "I know this is going to sound as if I'm cruel and nasty but every fighter knows that's all part of the game."[55] Worldwide figures show that over 361 boxers have been killed since 1945. Since the Marquis of Queensbury Rules were introduced in 1884, over 500 boxers have died in the ring or as a result of boxing.

The British Medical Association, which has campaigned to have the sport banned, says that 70 per cent of professional boxers may suffer serious brain damage: "Our major concern is with the chronic brain damage associated with boxing." The most common cause of death is brain haemorrhage. The most common injuries are detached retinas and persistent neurological damage, the "punch drunk" syndrome, with slurred speech and lack of memory and co-ordination affecting 20 per cent of older boxers. The BMA's Dr Paul Cundy said studies in the USA detected early signs of brain damage in amateurs who had boxed for less than two years: "The damage is cumulative. There is no repair process in the brain and when nerve fibre is broken the messages can't get through. Once brain cells have died they cannot be replaced."[56]

Being heavyweight champion of the world is seen as the greatest sporting accolade and rewarded with some of the highest prestige and pay anyone can receive. Mike Tyson in his heyday made $75 million in 1996, to top the Forbes Rich List. So a few black men make millions and some get killed as an immediate result. This is a cruel sport that should be outlawed at least on television, because publicity is the lifeblood of the sport. One reason for its pull for working-class men is because it is seen as one way out of the poverty trap.

The obstacles to a ban are not only the managers, promoters and TV companies who make a lot of money. "The state takes its cut whether the promoter makes money or loses money and whether the fighter wins or loses," manager and promoter Don Majesky is reported as saying.[57] Even promoters of this sport have their difficult moments defending it, as Frank Warren admitted: "There are times when you ask yourself whether you should be part of this business.... When Jim Murray died on a show I promoted in Glasgow, I couldn't look his mom and dad in the eye and defend boxing." Warren has been close to other boxers who suffered terrible injuries, but he insists: "the sport will continue until men have nothing left to fight for, and without making a political issue out of it, until the young men who go into it because they have no life or other prospects are given some by the politicians who want to ban it."[58] Far from banning it, one Cabinet minister advocated bringing it back in schools, as a way to teach children discipline and some schools already have done so. Fight clubs have proliferated, with the Amateur Boxing Association boasting an increase in numbers of competitive boxers from 7,000 to 18,000 and over 100 new clubs in the three years to the end of 2008.[59] At a time of increased loss of life through street violence the last thing we need is for the stereotyping of men as violent to be on the increase; it is time for a ban on this cruel sport.

## Homophobia

The fear of same-sex closeness is key to the oppression of men. Homophobia is engendered in the first instance not by anything to do with sex but by boys daring not to conform to the male stereotype of fighting, being tough and putting girls down. To deviate from what is considered "natural" masculine behaviour creates difficulties for boys refusing to play the game. Men cannot fight for their liberation and at the same time oppress other men for their sexuality. Oppressive societies depend on men fearing and not trusting one another. How else would men be prepared to kill other men in wartime on request? Taking a stand on gay men's right to be different is important for us all in the fight to end oppression. If we tolerate the oppression of any one group we make the argument for the oppression of other groups, including our own.

There is a lot of pressure preventing men from forming meaningful same-sex relationships; it happens for women too, but not in the same way, since there is a little more tolerance of close female friendships. Noticing how the pressure for men not to have close same-sex friendships affects the way men relate is important in defeating homophobia. We cannot end the oppression of men if gay men are oppressed because of their sexuality.

**Exercise: Learning homophobia.** What was it like for you growing up with close male friends? What was the attitude of the people around you towards gay men?

## My story: Challenging homophobia

When my friend John was terminally ill I regularly visited him in hospital. He had been very ill for a number of years and I often looked out for him as he had no family close by. On my visits to the hospital there was a suspicion sometimes from the nurses about our relationship. One nurse even asked point blank about the nature of our relationship. I guess it was unusual for them to see a black man taking an interest in an older white man.

I also faced this same kind of pressure when on holiday with my eldest son. One day we were travelling on a train and two gay men, also on holiday, made the assumption that we too were a gay couple. Later, in the holiday resort where we stayed, I was asked for a dance by a woman at the disco. I declined the invitation simply because I did not like the music. As we made the way back to our rooms after the disco finished, one of the women in passing with her partner said: "Don't do anything we wouldn't do." Her remark surprised me a bit because my son and I look so alike I thought it would be obvious to anyone that we were related.

Interrupting homophobia in our everyday life is important in raising awareness about the oppression of gay men. Travelling late one night I witnessed a homophobic attack on a train in London. Four young black men who joined the train were taunting three gay men in the carriage where I was sitting. They flicked their lighters as they sang the lyrics of a popular homophobic ragga artist, which included the lines "burn them". When they began throwing cushions at the men I stood to intervene. I could see they were high and I was a bit worried that my intervention might start a fight. I tried to reason with them in a non-aggressive tone but they were mostly deaf to this. I had to be more assertive; I even contemplated, with some trepidation, hitting the leader, who was about the age of one of my sons. The youngest of the group, out of respect I think, appealed to his two friends to "Listen to the man". His pleas made little difference to them so I had to be more forceful, getting between them and the gay men. The abuse eventually stopped when they reached their destination and got off the train. After they left, I encouraged the gay men to report the incident, offering myself as a witness.

Not long after this, I objected to the same homophobic song being played at a private party. When the DJ with the support of others insisted on playing it, I left. On another occasion, when another homophobic song was played at a Guyanese dance, I approached DJ Tafawa and said how disappointed I was, explaining why, and he immediately pulled it. I could not party to music whose lyrics contribute to the persecution and deaths of gay men in Jamaica. With little or no protection from the government many have fled the country of their birth.

In Britain one in five gay people have suffered attacks with "beatings and sexual assault to persistent harassment and insults often from neighbours and workmates". [60] Most of the prejudice about gay men is learnt at an early age; getting over the effects of the socialization requires going back to those early memories and seeing the misinformation for what it is.

**Exercise: Unlearning homophobia.** What messages did you receive about gay/lesbian relationships? What would you need to overcome to form close same-sex relationships?

## Men are good

Imagine what it would be like to hear more stories about the good things men do, rather the bad things that are mostly reported. For some time I have searched for good news about men. It has taken years to compile a few stories from newspapers and TV. Often the "good" stories are of men giving their lives to save others — like the grandfather who sacrificed himself to save his grandson and his dog when they were caught below cliffs in a fast-rising tide; he helped the boy and dog on to a ledge but there was no room for him and he died in the freezing water. [61] Or the husband who died trying to save his drowning wife as the middle-aged couple was "dragged away by the fast running tide on the Norfolk Broads". [62] There was also the 84-year-old pensioner who "died as he tried to defend his wife from intruders".[63] On a softer note there was the rag-trade millionaire who died at 92 leaving $90 million of his fortune to "be divided among 383 people named in his will"; one benefactor said: "He was just the kindest, most loving person you could imagine."[64] Then there is Bill Gates, chairman of Microsoft, giving $750 million in what "ranks as one of the largest donations made by a living philanthropist." The money was for an alliance working to make vaccines available to some of the poorest children in the world. Gates was reported as saying: "Today, a child's access to life-saving vaccines too often depends on where he or she lives in the world, and that's unacceptable."[65] Another good story was of a "Santa" who gave out money to the needy at Christmas time over a number of years; when he was too ill to do it himself, he paid someone to hand out the cash.

> **Exercise: Men are good.** Think/talk about your story of a good man you know personally.

We have looked at the oppression of men; now let us turn to the oppression of women.

# CHAPTER THREE

............................

# WOMEN'S LIBERATION

The state-sanctioned oppression of women over thousands of years has left men with oppressive patterns of behaviour towards women, passed on from one generation to the next, in the name of tradition, religion, custom or culture. Through violence and fear of violence the subordination of women was enforced by the founding fathers of modern society. Defeating domestic violence will mean exposing and eradicating patriarchal rule.

From my experience of working with perpetrators I believe that sexism is one of the key factors in men's violence to women. There is nothing new in this; feminists have long argued the case, even before Francis Power Cobbe addressed the issue in parliament. In an article entitled "Wife torture in England", she argued that a solution to domestic violence could only be found by addressing the "widely accepted notion of women's inferiority."[1] Parliament responded by enacting the Matrimonial Causes Act of 1878. However, from experience we know that legislation, though helpful, is not enough to change behaviour. Sexism is deep-rooted social conditioning and because of its pervasiveness men may not be aware of their oppressive attitude and behaviour towards women. They have come to accept the notion that women are inferior to men as something that is "natural".

The belief that men must be in control of women is a key factor in men's violence towards women. Most of the male perpetrators I have worked with used violence to enforce the subordination of their partner, if she did not "do as she was told". They felt responsible for correcting any behaviour of their partner's that they did not approve of. This could be anything from the cooking, washing, cleaning, how they dressed, who their friends were, what they did or did not do; in fact, it could be anything. The socialization for men to take charge begins very early and it is not uncommon to hear departing fathers telling their sons to look after their mothers - as if the women could not look after themselves. These types of messages leave boys believing that they are expected to be in charge, as men. In many overtly patriarchal societies this is taken very seriously, with sons regarded as the head of the household when the father is away. This undermines women and reinforces the sexist conditioning for boys

Women need liberation because they are forced to live limited lives, are seen as less than, and are often denied the same opportunities as men. As we have seen in the previous chapter, women are particularly vulnerable to rape in times of war, but it is not only in wartime that women are raped. In so-called peace-time millions of women are raped or sexually abused each day. Research shows that in the USA alone a woman is raped every 6 minutes.[2] In the UK the figure is 1 in 20 women raped and many more sexually assaulted. That the majority of rape happens in the home, and mostly by a known male, underscores how unsafe women are in society. Men must put an end to this outrage if they are ever to reclaim their humanity.

One of the expectations of women is that they will become mothers and do most of the caring. This expectation to have children puts a great deal of pressure on women to bear children to prove they are "real" women and is oppressive for the many women who choose not to or cannot have babies for whatever reasons. Women's work in the home is valued less, if at all, and women are expected to do any caring that is required. This is very limiting and oppressive.

The feminist movement has fought long and hard to end gender discrimination. There have been notable successes but the fight for equality is far from over. Patriarchal rule on the whole benefits all men; but it is a tiny minority who are hugely rewarded financially and politically by the subordination of women. Defeating patriarchy will require fighting at both the personal and political levels.

**The Personal.** What is done in our personal lives reflects on our political/ public activity and should not be separated. Feminists have long recognized the importance of working on the personal as well as the political in attaining true liberation. If politicians behave without integrity and fairness in their personal lives how can we trust them in the public sphere? It is not acceptable for anyone to take a public stand against domestic violence or racism, for example, and in their private lives behave contrary to what they preach. It is only by working on the personal that it is possible to change deeply held oppressive patterns of behaviour. Pretence is no substitute for deep change, and shortcomings will be sooner or later exposed, as happened to a senior policeman who denied being racist yet during the same televised interview used derogatory racist language. Working on your personal history of sexism/racism or other oppressive material is important if you are to recover from the effects of any mistreatment and begin the unlearning of oppressive behaviour. Unlearning sexism is crucial in bringing about an end to patriarchy. Women also have work to do here, for they too have internalized the sexist conditioning of patriarchal rule.

**The Political.** Our world is shaped by politics; we cannot hope to end oppression without changing the political structures that encourage and support oppressive practices. Patriarchal rule was established with the use of propaganda and violence. The religions, the philosophies, the educators, the cultural artists, etc, were all encouraged and rewarded in their efforts to convince everyone that women were naturally inferior to men and that the use of violence was natural to men. We live in a society saturated in sexism; none of us escape the conditioning that leaves us believing men to be more important than women. Though this conditioning is responsible for the sexism exhibited by men, the notion that men are inherently sexist must be continually challenged as part of the strategy for ending sexism.

The lies propagated over millennia about the true nature of women have left many people believing that women are inferior to men. The propaganda continues unabated today, in the many books and theories supporting male hegemony and pedalling the notion that men and women might as well be from different planets and need different "rules" to live by. Every time we accept the notion that we are so fundamentally different, we succumb to the belief that women, because of their gender, are rightly treated differently. Often "different" translates as "inferior" to men in the things that really matter, so this thinking encourages those determined to keep women subjugated. Women have long recognized that to challenge the notion of women's inferiority is important in ending the oppression. As bell hooks relates, in 1852 a man at the second annual convention of the women's rights movement in Akron, Ohio, spoke against equal rights for women. He argued that "woman was too weak to perform her share of manual labour-that she was innately the physical inferior to man." The white middle-class audience was stunned by this, but the black abolitionist and former slave Sojourner Truth quickly rebuffed his argument, addressing the audience:

*Well, children, whar dar is so much racket dar must be something out o'kilter. I tink dat 'twixt de niggers of de Souf and de women at de Norf all a talking 'bout rights, de white man will be in a fix pretty soon. But what's all dis here talkin' 'bout? Dat man ober dar say that women needs to be helped into carriages, and lifted ober ditches, and to have de best places…and ain't I a woman? Look at me! Look at my arm! …I have plowed, and planted and gathered into barns, and no man could head me - and ain't I a woman? I could work as much as any man (when I could get it), and bear the lash as well - and ain't I a woman? I have borne five children and I seen 'em most sold off into slavery, and when I cried out with a mother's grief, none but Jesus hear - and ain't I a woman?"*[3]

It is doubtful that one of the white middle-class women could have made such a stout defence at the time and this underlines the case for a movement to end sexism that is also working to end classism and racism. The oppressive society survives by dividing us in every possible way - by race, class, gender, size, age, religion, etc - and strategies to end oppression will fail if these issues are ignored.

Almost all religions have played a role in propagating the idea that women are fundamentally different from and implicitly inferior to men. Only recently the Pope warned against feminists "blurring the biological difference between men and women".[4] No one can deny that there are biological differences between men and women, but these are of little consequence when compared to the many similarities of the sexes. The differences are generally exaggerated by those determined to justify the oppression women.

We share the same attributes: women are strong, men are strong; men are caring, women are caring; men are intelligent, women are intelligent, and so on. Yes, women may be better at caring, but this is a result of centuries of conditioning rather than being biologically determined – to know this, we need only take note of cultures such as the Arapesh in New Guinea, where men stay at home to care for the children while the women do the hunting and gathering. We can also note the women who show little caring, and occasionally even kill their own children, to recognize as false the arguments about women being biologically determined to provide care. The labelling of one gender with a particular attribute is often an excuse to oppress them. This is how "strength" has been used to put men on the frontline of wars and women have been overburdened with "caring" responsibilities in the home.

To stereotype woman as home-maker and mother helps perpetuate the idea that all women are biologically destined for these roles. This is the propaganda of the patriarchs that would keep women oppressed by taking away their right to choose. It is an ongoing battle for feminists everywhere. Not long ago, the Pope joined forces with some of the most oppressive patriarchs to forge an alliance to deny women the right to choose what to do with their bodies. In Nicaragua, after a campaign by the Catholic Church, the government passed legislation "to outlaw all forms of abortion, including operations to save a pregnant woman's life".[5] At the same time the largest Protestant group in the USA urged their followers to "submit" to their husbands, ordering that the man should, "provide and protect and lead his family".[6] They would take us back to the worst days of patriarchal rule. Even in hunter/gatherer societies women were not seen as dependants; there was more a sense of "separate but equal" and often women did the most basic provision, by gathering and hunting small game.[7]

Men often do not understand what sexism is about as their understanding of gender issues is gleaned from the popular press, whose hostility to feminism has served to alienate most women from identifying with it and made men hostile to the women's liberation movement.

Understanding the disadvantages that women face in society is crucial in ending the oppression. Some feminists question whether it makes sense to talk of "oppression" at all. Gerda Lerner argues that "subordination" may be a better word to describe the situation for women, since oppression implies victimization, and that makes us "conceptualise women-as-a-group primarily as victims." And that, "while all women have been victimised in certain aspects of their lives and some at certain times more than others, women are structured into society in such a way that they are both subjects and agents".[8] Whichever words are used to describe the situation for women in the world today, without a doubt women are disadvantaged in almost every aspect of their lives. For many, "oppression" may better reflect the reality of their existence. These are some facts of women's oppression:

## Politics

Men still have a monopoly on political power because women historically have been excluded from politics; a current culture of unsocial hours still makes it harder for women to participate fully. As a result women are vastly under-represented in the UK's political process, despite the suffragettes fighting a long and hard campaign for women to win the vote. One seasoned campaigner for votes for women, Emily Davidson, spent time in prison doing hard labour, where she was "almost killed by prison authorities", before paying the ultimate price for her beliefs in 1913, when she was run over by a racehorse as she protested by running with the suffragette banner onto the Epsom racecourse track. Women were eventually granted the vote in 1916. Some countries still deny women the vote and many reluctantly give in to any kind of power-sharing, as evidenced in Kuwait, which recently admitted the first woman to Parliament "over the shouts of Islamists and traditionalists opposed to women in politics".[9]

The number of women in politics is increasing, but not fast enough; at the present rate it will take 200 years for women to have parity in Parliament in England.[10] Where there has been positive discrimination the numbers have gone up dramatically. For example, in 2003 Rwanda had the highest proportion of women in government in the world at 48.9 per cent, beating Sweden into second with 45.3per cent of seats. This compares with Britain, ranked 50th in the world, with 17.9 per cent in government, and the USA ranked 60 with a mere 14.3 per cent.

**Education**

Great effort has gone into casting women as less intelligent than men over the centuries and the propaganda continues unabated with recent claims by two researchers (who had previously claimed that white people were smarter than black people) that men are at least five IQ points smarter than women. The findings have been dismissed, as "utter hogwash" by Dr Steve Blinkhorn, an expert on intelligence testing.[11]

Although women have historically been prevented from having an education (and this is still true in many countries around the world today), where girls have been given equal opportunity to have an education they have often outperformed boys. In the UK women in higher education now make up 57 per cent of the student population, with the gulf growing, year on year and they have more passes too.[12] Claims that women are intellectually inferior to men[13] can only be from those that would send women to the stake if they could.

## Equal-Pay Discrimination

The capitalist system has deliberately manipulated gender issues to facilitate its exploitation of workers. Keep women at home to produce the future work force and have them service the worker for free has served capitalism very well. Even when women joined the work force, their work was valued less and paid less.

Women have struggled long for equal pay and the struggle goes on despite the Trades Union Congress backing equal pay for women for nearly 90 years before Barbara Castle, on the 42nd attempt was able to force equal pay legislation on to the statute books in 1975. Some 34 years later, women are still waiting to be paid the same as men for doing the same work, despite the Labour government giving companies five years to adjust to the legislation, at the time. The government was accused of undermining the spirit of the law in 1993, by blocking moves to simplify them; at the time they claimed that reforms would cost jobs.[14] This resistance to treating women with equality persists, as the present New Labour government, finds it unnecessary to enforce a pay audit on companies; trusting that companies will do this voluntarily. This ploy to yet further delay payment runs against all reality, as a survey, by the private-sector union Amicus found that only 50 out of the 6,000 firms questioned, were prepared to carry out equal pay audits.[15] It is an injustice that the average man in a full-time job still earns £100 per week more than the average woman, according to the office of national statistics report in 2005. This despite more women now being better qualified than men.

Apart from equal pay, women face discrimination in getting the top jobs in almost every sphere of employment. The *Guardian's* annual executive pay survey in 2003 revealed that out of 597 fulltime directors only 15 were women. Only one was a chief executive and she earned half the average £1.7m package for a typical chief executive.[16] Departments that should be exemplary in upholding the law are as guilty as any other: of 12 judges in the House of Lords only one was a woman, Dame Brenda Hale (who made legal history as the first woman judge). The situation for women seems to be worsening, with Britain slipping down the world league table on gender equality three years in a row "and is now ranked 13th out of 130 countries in terms of women's pay and work opportunities, political power, health and education."[17]

Legislation is important in bringing about change, but legislation alone is not enough to change attitudes. There has to be a will for change, before any change can take place. It takes years of concerted, committed action to unlearn the generations of sexist conditioning affecting behaviour. The slow pace of change is a result of the sexism that persists in the men with the power to make a real difference. Had women been in charge of implementing the legislation, equality of pay would have been a reality ages ago. The sexism that stops this legislation being implemented costs women billions of pounds in earnings and loss of prestige each year.

Men are often unaware of what sexism is all about, so let us look at some of the concepts.

**Sexism** at its very basic is the mistreatment of women solely because of their sex. This mistreatment comes in all guises: a look, a word, a suggestion, a thought, an action or inaction. Sexism is life-threatening; many women die because of its effects. It is sexism when women are sentenced more harshly than men for the same offences. The Home Office acknowledged that "magistrates' courts used custody three times more frequently for women in 2002 than in 1994, yet the 'nature and seriousness of their offending' has not been getting worse."[18]

Men have been conditioned for millennia to think of and treat women as inferior. They are often unaware of the hurt and damage they cause. When the mistreatment becomes endemic in the society it is regarded as cultural. This can have devastating consequences, as shockingly demonstrated by two of the world's most populous countries. In India, where boys are valued more highly than girls, over 500,000 girl babies are selectively aborted each year. China, where infant girls were simply left in the woods to die, now faces a serious shortage of women; in the year 2003, 117 boys were born for every 100 girls, compared with a global average of 105 to 100. As a result of the social pressures being stored up, the Chinese government is attempting to rectify the imbalance by offering to pay a premium for those producing baby girls.[19] In parts of Africa, millions of girls have their genitalia mutilated in the name of culture. A UNICEF survey found that 97 per cent of married women in Egypt had been circumcised and half of all girls aged 10-18.20 The recent death of a 12-year-old girl who had been genitally mutilated has forced the Egyptian government to ban this procedure.

**Unaware/covert sexism** affects all men. Western philosophy is grounded in sexism; Aristotle, Darwin and Freud, who have greatly influenced the way we think, were all sexist in their thinking. It is impossible for men to grow up in patriarchal society and not be affected by the male supremacist thinking and the belief that men are superior to women. This belief is continually propagated and is responsible for much of the discrimination women face today.

An example of unwitting sexism is when men simply don't hear women's opinions expressed. Most men are not even aware that they do this because they are conditioned to not take women seriously; as a result they continually interrupt women and ignore their opinions. Many men only hear a woman's opinion when it is taken and expressed by a male, who invariably fails to acknowledge where the idea originated. Having low expectations of women and seeing them as sex objects are deeply ingrained in men, who are often unaware that their deeds and thoughts are influenced by this thinking on a daily basis.

**Aware/overt sexism** is when men act out their feelings of superiority over women, and believe that they are right in so doing. Some men treat women as inferior because they have the power as males to do so. They deliberately put women down, and think it right to use violence if women refuse to accept this notion of them being superior. They see women as sex objects and treat them as such by, for example, using their bodies to sell anything from cars to cat food. It is overt sexism when women are charged more for cars.[21]

It is sexism that values boy babies more than girls or destroys them in preference to boys. It is overt sexism when men attack women and burn them with acid just because they try to get an education or that women receive death threats for speaking out about their oppression.[22]

One of the key places we learn sexism is in the home. Gender socialization begins from the moment babies are put into blue or pink and it continues for most of our lives. Because the conditioning starts so young we are left with patterns of behaviour that are very deep-seated. There are ways we can begin to challenge and change the sexist conditioning but they require concerted, conscious action if they are to be changed. This is best done with some support and was the reasoning behind many of the women's groups forming to challenge sexism in the 1960s and 1970s. Unlearning gender conditioning is a good place to start undermining these patterns of behaviour. Some men's groups also exist that work at challenging sexism.

> **Exercise: Unlearning sexism.** If you have never cooked a meal or put up a shelf, now is a good time to start learning. Plan one of these activities and get support with it, if you don't know where to begin.

Sexism is learned behaviour that serves the interests of the oppressive society but it can be unlearned. Patriarchy has always manipulated men to participate in mistreating women, but not all men collude with this. A great example is John Stuart Mill, who challenged sexism in 1869 by asking in his book *The Subjection of Women* why one half of the human race should be subordinated to the other.[23] Walter Rodney in *The History of the Guyanese Working People* shows how the British colonial masters tried to manipulate the recently freed slave men into breaking a strike by emancipated women. They chided the men for not being able to control "their" women, with the hope that the men would show solidarity with other men and force the women back to work. This tactic backfired; with memories of enslavement by white men still fresh, the men instead joined the women in their strike action for better pay and conditions.[24]

I promised that you wouldn't have to do anything I wouldn't do, so let us take a look at how the socialization for sexism affects us personally.

**My story: Learning sexism**

As a young man in my early teens I had a lot of time to "lime" on the streets with the boys in the afternoons. This is where misogyny reigned supreme. We mostly talked about girls and bragged about our sexual encounters with them. It was not unusual for these stories to be far-fetched, as we tried to impress one another with our conquests. Sometimes the conversations would vary from the usual, with arguments/discussions about male supremacy. One of the dilemmas posed was: if you had a boy and a girl child and could only afford to educate one, which one would you educate? The argument for educating the boy almost always won the day, on the grounds that the girl would marry and leave the family, with a resulting loss of investment. We also discussed equality of the sexes, with the Bible being quoted to uphold male superiority, this proposition again winning majority support. A few agreed with equality of the sexes, which was a novel idea at the time and one I am proud to say I argued for.

But this was no debating society and we primarily gathered to "interfere" with young women as they passed by. We behaved with utter disregard for their feelings and cat-called, whistled and generally molested females who were unaccompanied by a male. We saw nothing wrong in having a bit of fun at their expense. Friendship with girls were frowned upon and closely scrutinized by other boys. There was no point in having a girlfriend if you were not at least trying to have sex with her. As a matter of fact we were put down if we had a girlfriend and were not having sex; you were deemed a "blocker", preventing other boys from getting at her. There was enormous pressure brought to bear to disclose the nature of a relationship with any girl. Not surprisingly, we often lied to relieve this pressure. Any show of affection, such as giving gifts or holding hands, was frowned on and invited ridicule for being "soft".

Relationships were often portrayed as a battle of the sexes and as men we had to get the upper hand. We were all out to "score", and lying and cheating was the order of the day. Women were generally regarded as sex objects to be conquered, by any means short of rape. We lived by the saying, "all's fair in love and war". I remember this was the justification I used for some really bad behaviour towards girls. I hang my head in shame.

Apart from having to contend with sexist conditioning, there is also the gender conditioning that usually serves to reinforce sexism. In this I have been a little fortunate.

## My story: More about sexism

I was the third son of five boys in a family of seven children. My mother gave birth to four boys in succession before a girl was born into the family. This had a profound effect on the gender socialization that we boys received. I suspect things would have been very different had we had an older sister.

My dad's work took him away from home for long spells, which left Mom to raise us children on her own for a lot of the time. Just keeping us clean was hard work, as like most other families around us we had no running water in the home, much less a washing-machine. The work was just too much for Mom to keep us active boys in clean clothes. So at an early age we had to learn to wash our own clothes by hand. This was one of the hardest jobs for us, as we also had to fetch the water from a standpipe some distance away. We also had other jobs, such as keeping the house and yard clean, caring for plants, ironing, washing dishes and doing the most embarrassing potty-run to the latrine in the mornings. It is no wonder that I am still an early riser. Sadly, we were not taught how to cook. I suppose my mother could not afford to have cooking disasters with the family meal. However, I had the idea that I could take care of myself and quickly learnt to cook when I moved away from home.

Many of my friends, in a similar situation, were socialized in the same way but for those with older sisters things were very different. They never had to do housework and probably got the message that it was "women's work". A lot depended on our parents' attitude; one of my friends who had many sisters was good at all the things his sisters could do, including plaiting hair. He was the second child in a big family of girls so had to learn to help with this task too. I always envied him being able to plait his girlfriend's hair. As boys growing up, we prided ourselves on the fact that we did not "need" a woman to take care of us.

> **Exercise: Unlearning sexism.** What was gender socialization like for you? Stop and take time to think, talk or write about it. How does it affect your behaviour today? What do you need to change?

Notice how we are pressured to conform to the gender stereotypes created for us. Boys get called "sissy" or some derogatory term if they show an interest in things deemed female. Girls who dare to step out of the conditioning for their caring role get called "tomboys", or whatever name is used in your particular culture, as a way of forcing them to conform to the stereotype for girls. There is immense pressure in the home, school and on the streets, from peers and older boys and girls, to conform to the stereotypical roles assigned to us.

An analysis of children's picture books found that women were overwhelmingly portrayed as dependent, passive, working in the home or not working at all and as preferring indoor activities.[25] It is important to note how this negative stereotyping of women affects the way women are perceived. Women who accept these stereotypes can end up living very limited lives; many men accept these messages and in their relationships expect their partners to act out these stereotypical roles. Similarly, for men to step out of their "roles" challenges the sexist stereotypes created for us and is one way to undermine sexist conditioning.

## Session time:

It has been some time now since you have started working at stopping your violent patterns of behaviour. What is the situation for you now? Have you been able to stop your violence? How do you feel about yourself? What do you notice has changed in you?

I want to take some time to appreciate your efforts for staying with the journey to stop your violence and reclaim your true self. Are you still in the relationship and how is it going? If the situation is still difficult, just remember that you must be patient. You cannot expect your partner to believe that you will never hit again because you have started using this book. You can expect some criticism and possibly anger at your efforts to change; they are perhaps angry that you did not make these efforts before now. You may be tested in your resolve to change, so keep making the decision and commitment each day to change your behaviour. Remember, when you hit, you would have let yourself down yet again but this is no reason to give up trying to change; it is a time to work even harder at defeating this pattern. Always bear in mind that violence is learned behaviour that can be unlearned. You can do it. I am right with you in this battle to have a better life, not only for yourself but also for the loved ones around you; even the ones who are sceptical that you can ever change. You have to prove them wrong in this. My heart goes out to you and to your efforts to make this a better world for us all.

## Language and Liberation

Language has always been used as a tool of oppression; this is one of the reasons why so much of the language used by the state apparatus is difficult for most citizens to understand. It is not meant for the majority, this is why people employ those trained in the use of the language to represent them in legal matters. Using language to oppress is nowhere clearer than in the enslavement of a people. During the era of the Trans-Atlantic Slave Trade the enslaved Africans were prevented from speaking in their own languages under threat of severe punishment, or even death. Afraid of rebellion being plotted in a language they could not understand, the slave owners enforced harsh punishment, including cutting out tongues, for any of the enslaved heard speaking their native languages. The oppressors not only denied them their language but imposed their own language on the oppressed people, resulting in the official language of many former colonies being that of their oppressors.

Similarly, sexist language is used as a tool to undermine women. This is one of the ways women were excluded from historical (after all it is his-story we are talking about) accounts - as though they were not worth a *mention*. Though feminists have fought for language to be used more inclusively, much of the language printed is still addressed to a male audience, and unsurprisingly is found wanting. The popular press delights in deriding the "political correctness" of those trying to bring about change in the way language is used to oppress.

Roy Hattersley, former deputy of the Labour Party, made the point about the use of language very poignantly when he described an encounter with Senator Robert Kennedy. They were setting out on a car journey to meet Bayard Rustin, the great US civil rights leader, when Senator Kennedy asked if anybody knew whether Rustin preferred to be called a Black (with a capital B) American, a "person of colour" or Afro-Caribbean. None of them had the answer so the senator sent someone to find out. "Irritated beyond good manners by the constant delays, I offered the opinion that it was easy to be too sensitive about such details. Senator Kennedy addressed me in the strange nasal voice, which was common to his whole family. *"If your grandfather had been a slave, you would be sensitive about what people call you."*[26]

The use of derogatory language to whip up the military has been a tool of the armed forces for centuries. If people are dehumanized with the use of words then it is much easier to kill or harm them. The military have recognized that it is easier for servicemen to envisage killing a "gook", "kong", "frog", or whatever word they find to dehumanize the enemy, and this knowledge is exploited in preparing men to go into battle.

Interrupting any sexist and derogatory language being used by perpetrators in a counselling session is important. If you talk or even think about your partner in derogatory terms you are more likely to harm them. For male perpetrators the words "bitch" or "cunt" are most often used in this context. If you use such language you need to stop. You only have to think back to your incidents of violence to notice that it usually starts with abusive language. Deciding never to use abusive sexist language is important in breaking the cycle of violence. Let us look at some of the derogatory language used.

**Exercise for women and men: Recognizing sexist language.** Draw two columns with a heading for men and women, then list the words you have heard used to describe men and women. Notice, first, which is the bigger list. Then notice which group has the most words used to degrade.

It is easy to spot the double standards. A man with many women: a stud - a relatively kind word. A woman with many lovers: the derogatory whore, bitch or slut. The most used and most offensive - "cunt" - is the word that is most attacking of women and likely to start a fight if used against a male. This is a derogatory word for the female sexual organ or vagina and it demeans women. Deciding not to use such words is the first step in rejecting sexism. Most of this language is learnt at a young age, so interrupting its use in young ones is important.

**Exercise: Breaking the habit.** Make a list of the sexist language you use and need to stop using. Find a way to monitor your use with rewards for compliance and penalties for using them. For example, one couple had a jar into which a fixed amount was paid, as a penalty for non-compliance.

Men are not inherently sexist but sexism is installed at a very early age. Patriarchy depends on men accepting male supremacist thinking, and given the centuries of oppression of women it is not surprising that so many men hold the belief that they are superior to women. Sexist attitudes are being passed on to men from one generation to the next and are deeply ingrained. At the same time, girls are being socialized to accept a subordinate role. Studies show that by the age of five, children have already developed clear notions of what constitutes appropriate behaviour for men and women.[27] This early conditioning can make a difference to the kind of life chances available to women. If we discourage our daughters from taking part in all of the activities available to them as children, we teach them to accept a gender stereotyping that is oppressive of women. It is especially important that men encourage their girls in the same activities as their sons as one way of interrupting this sexist gender stereotyping. Boys can learn to bake cakes just as well as girls can learn to mend or fix things.

**Pornography.** This multi-billion industry, controlled mainly by men, is exploitative of women's bodies and does a great deal of damage to men and women who become addicted to its use. Pornography, like sport, consumerism and addictive substances, distracts us from changing the oppressive society we live in. A few of the men I have worked with were heavily addicted to pornography and recognized that its long-term use made it difficult for their sexual relationship with their partners.

Using women's bodies as objects to sell products serves to keep sex on our minds constantly. If men are continually bombarded with photographs of women's naked bodies everywhere, advertising objects from cars to cat food, should we be so surprised? When we have sex forced into our brains non-stop, we have little time to think about the oppressive society we live in and even less motivation to do anything to change it.

## Women and Violence

Surveys support a general perception that women are becoming more violent. Some researchers[28] blame the amount of violence shown on television and in films such as *GI Jane*, starring Demi Moore, serving to perpetrate a stereotype of violent women. A YWCA briefing report, *If Looks Could Kill: Young Women and Bullying*, claims: "Girls are now more involved in sustained bullying than boys and they have more fear of going to school."[29] It is crucial, in the name of equality of the sexes, to oppose the increasing socialization of women for violence, or we face the likelihood of a greater problem with domestic violence in the future.

In some societies, male and female stereotypes are now not as rigid as in the recent past. Although the socialization of women is still basically for a caring role, women make up more than half the workforce and a growing percentage of the armed forces and are increasingly expected to play an active role in armed combat. This right to kill is presented as an equalities issue worth fighting for. The oppressive society is expert at manipulating people to meet its needs. In World War 1, when women were needed for the war effort they were encouraged out of the home. Later, in response to a shortage of "jobs for the boys" returning from the war, women were pressured back into the home.

Women have always supported war efforts in a secondary role and without a doubt there is progress in breaking with a tradition that in World War 1 confined servicewomen mainly to secretarial, cooking and cleaning work, while in World War 2 they could be mechanics, drivers, photographers, bomb plotters or radio operators. This shows there has been a shift in thinking, but it cannot be regarded as progress when women are trained to be fighter pilots and targeted to make up the shortfall in male volunteers to kill or be killed in times of war.

### Internalized Sexism

If only women could be convinced of their inferior status then less effort would be needed to control them. Lerner argues: "Women have for millennia participated in the process of their own subordination because they have been psychologically shaped so as to internalize the idea of their own inferiority. The unawareness of their own history of struggle and achievement has been one of the major means of keeping women subordinate."[30]

One of the effects of centuries of sexism is that most women internalized the oppression. Experiments by Phillip Goldberg demonstrated that women have been thought to consider themselves the intellectual inferiors of men. In a series of exercises he gave women a number of scholarly articles to read and then to evaluate. An article they thought was written by a man they scored more highly than any they thought were written by women.[31]

One way to overcome the negative stereotyping of women is to familiarize ourselves with the many outstanding achievements of women in spite of all the obstacles they have placed before them. Having our own heroines is important in this. By reading books written by feminists we can learn a lot about the true nature of women.

One of the expectations put on women is that they have a civilizing influence on men. This notion, that men are brutes who somehow with the "soft touch" of women will become civilized, may be responsible for many women feeling responsible for the violence of their men. After all, if they had done their job of civilizing them there would be no violence. Admitting to the violence done to them is like admitting that they have failed in their job of civilizing their man - no wonder so many women remain silent about the violence for so long.

Women have had to develop survival skills because of the heavy oppression they faced during the formation of archaic states, in order to escape brutal punishment or even death. Most of these skills are about appeasing or pleasing men. Even if women were unhappy with the situation they had to pretend otherwise. As a result, "pretence" patterns were perfected as a key tool for women in manipulating men. These skills are no longer useful or necessary for women's survival in most countries but persist because of the early gender socialization. This is similar to the experience of enslaved Africans, who learned to accept their position to ensure the survival of their children, by deferring to the white slave master. These survival patterns of behaviour have persisted in some descendants of slaves and serve to support the institution of racism.

As women accepted the rule of men under patriarchy the process of internalization of sexism began. Once women internalized the oppression the behaviour patterns were passed on to daughters, to ensure their survival in a male dominated world. These patterns of behaviour would probably be called *choice*, but how many of the decisions about appearance and lifestyles are based on *real* choice as opposed to conditioning is debatable.

In countries where the oppression of women is deeply entrenched, domestic violence is even more prevalent, with women often accepting the abuse. A recent survey of countries found that 77 per cent of Ugandan women believe it is right for their husbands to beat them; it was 51 per cent for Zimbabwe, Turkmenistan 52 per cent, Nepal 29 per cent, and 40 per cent for Haiti.[32] These are also some of the poorest countries in the world. No figures were published for Western countries but this belief is also held here, if perhaps to a lesser extent.

A recent survey of 2,000 teenagers in Britain found that 43 per cent believed it acceptable for a boyfriend to get aggressive in certain circumstances, with 6 per cent of girls saying it was acceptable for a boy to hit his girlfriend. Some changes are happening in the developed world, as recent research has shown that self-esteem among females is on the increase, possibly because women are doing much better than men academically in some countries.

Interrupting the "internalization" of the oppression of women is an important step in defeating domestic violence. We cannot depend on states rooted in oppression to bring about change; we can begin to make a difference by undermining the gender conditioning that sustains this oppression. Making a habit of interrupting sexism whenever we have the opportunity will raise consciousness and help end the oppression. For men it may be something as simple as washing the dishes or clearing up at a social event. Notice how many women will still try to take this job away from men.

It takes courage to challenge gender conditioning, as the pressure to conform is so great. Try doing anything that is expected of the opposite sex and notice the pressure from both men and women to have you conform to the stereotypical role assigned to your gender. The overwhelming socialization for women is as caregivers; the pull to take care of men is overwhelming for some women. Some men exploit this and use women as a "sop" for all their problems. Having unloaded their burdens on women, some men then use it as an excuse for their bad behaviour, and expect the woman to "understand". This is most abusive and not helpful in building loving relationships based on equality. Men must seek professional help if they have deep-seated problems. Women must refuse to be treated as caregivers.

Internalized sexism works to undermine solidarity of women and still too many women are proud to say that they find it easier to have men friends — some have no girl friends. Books such as *Bitch* do not help the situation. The word "bitch" means she-dog, and the majority of people understand the implications of the word. Have you seen a bitch "on heat"? Men have used this sexist language to put women down for generations. When women start using it on themselves they have internalized the oppression, just as with black people and the word "nigger". This is not neutralizing the power of these words to offend, as some believe, but another way of colluding with the oppression. Celebrating the numerous occasions of celebrity "bitching" only serves to make us more suspicious and mistrustful of women. That type of publication just plays into the hands of the oppressive society, pretty much like the backward *Rules*; they make grand headlines and huge sales because they support patriarchal agenda.

## Men ending sexism

Well, I never said change would be easy, especially when dealing with deep-seated and long-held beliefs that we have been led to believe were true. Changing the attitude or behaviour of a lifetime requires concerted effort; old behaviour patterns will keep pulling us back to what we have been comfortable with for a long time. It is not your fault that we live in a society saturated in sexism, but you can choose to do something about challenging and changing the oppression by overcoming the sexist patterns of behaviour you have learnt. Men can never be truly happy while they behave in an oppressive manner to half of the world's population. Men owe it to themselves to end the oppression of women, not to "save" women, but to give themselves a chance for a better life. Men can make a huge difference, as bell hooks argues: "Since men are the primary agents maintaining and supporting sexism and sexist oppression, they can only be successfully eradicated if men are compelled to assume responsibility for transforming their consciousness and the consciousness of society as a whole."[33]

Men need to be involved in the struggle to end the oppression of women, not to let their control patterns try to take over the struggle from women, but to give support to the struggle. Understanding how sexism works is important in defeating it.

## My story: Understanding sexism

When I was first accused of being sexist by one of my political comrades, I could not accept what I was hearing. We were out drinking and I convinced myself that maybe she had had too much to drink. Now, Andaiye is one of the smartest women I know, so when she accused me again on another occasion, I had to stop and think hard about it. I had always believed in equality of the sexes, so how could she accuse me of being sexist? This was very confusing for me, and I felt hurt by the accusation.

I respected her thinking enough to decide that there must be some truth in what she was saying. After all, she had been right in most things we had discussed politically or otherwise. So I decided to find out exactly what she was talking about; maybe I didn't quite get what this "sexism" thing was all about. Fortunately, my partner at the time was a feminist who had quite a few books on "women's liberation", so I began reading. I was in for a rude awakening, it was as if a new world opened up to me and it dawned on me that I was as sexist as you could get.

I decided to do something about that sexism and I am still working on it. This is an ongoing process, not something you can understand or change overnight. A bit like unlearning racism, you have to keep working at it all of the time. The sexist conditioning is so deep it requires constant vigilance to overcome it. Recognizing sexism for what it is and learning how to interrupt it in yourself and in others will help you to overcome the conditioning.

I want to pay tribute to some of the women whose scholarship, activism and awareness have made a huge difference to the person I am today. Andaiye I have mentioned, who was the first to challenge my sexism in a way that I had to listen and take action. Sally (mother of three of my children), for her collection of feminist books and her many challenges from which I learnt a lot in the early days. Women writers and activists continue to inspire me. One of the first, who really started me on the road of political activism was Angela Davis; when she was the most wanted woman by the FBI, I looked at her "wanted" poster and decided that this beautiful woman could not be responsible for the crimes they accused her of; as a result I started reading more about the struggle against racist oppression in the USA. Her book *Women, Race and Class* moved me to another level of consciousness. Then came bell hooks with *Ain't I a Woman*, written at age 19, signalling that a great intellect was about to be unleashed on the political scene. Her book *Feminist Theory: from margin to center* empowered me as a man to stand firm in the fight against sexism in the knowledge that "feminism is natural to all people who love freedom". I want a world where men will rush out to have coffee with a feminist in her lifetime.[34] Maya Angelou, who knows "why the caged bird sings"; for her books and poetry, and her warm hug that will stay with me for ever. Andrea Dworkin, for her thinking on pornography. Alice Walker for *The Color Purple*. Gerda Lerner for filling many gaps with *The Creation of Patriarchy*. Many thanks to Claire Rayner, for her thoughts at a crucial stage of the process in helping me make a decision to write this book for all perpetrators of domestic violence. To Barbara Love, for her commitment to Black Liberation and her support in my personal growth and development. I could go on and on but will stop here and simply acknowledge my mother and all the many women friends and lovers who have made a real difference in my life.

Men can begin to challenge sexism by having relationships with women that are not based on sex. This is not easy, as men have been discouraged from having friendships with women from an early age. Being called "momma's boy" is responsible for the early separation from mothers. Men must reclaim that first relationship if they are to make a difference. The sexist socialization that branded boys "sissies" for having friendships with girls or participating in things deemed feminine add to the difficulties in making relationships with women, but these obstacles are not insurmountable.

Girls are under similar pressure to not have close friendships with boys, and doing "boy" things often landed them with the label "tomboy". In some overtly patriarchal countries girls are still prevented from taking part in athletic events and are physically attacked for attempting to do so. Patriarchy undermines us from forming relationships based on equality of the sexes and every time we challenge this thinking we bring not only men's liberation but also the liberation of women closer.

Men owe a great deal to the feminist movement for speaking out about their oppression and developing a concept of liberation. By developing a movement that challenges the system, they have shown men the way to fight for their liberation. It is not so hard for people to understand that men too are oppressed and that the two liberation movements are not incompatible. "The system of patriarchy is a historic construct; it has a beginning; it will have an end. Its time seems to have nearly run its course — it no longer serves the needs of men or women and in its inextricable linkage to militarism, hierarchy, and racism it threatens the very existence of life on earth."[35] We can begin the work of ending sexism by reclaiming our relationships with the opposite sex. It is in everyone's interest to put an end to the oppression of women. Men would be able to have better lives as they are no longer trapped in gender roles, having to feel responsible for supporting women economically or giving their lives protecting women and children. The stakes are high: "A feminist world-view will enable women and men to free their minds from patriarchal thought and practice and at last to build a world free of dominance and hierarchy, a world that is truly human."[36]

# CHAPTER FOUR

........................

# GIVING UP ADDICTIONS

Working with men to stop their violent behaviour has meant looking at all aspect of their lives to see which contributing factors were responsible for the general unhappiness that caused much of their bad behaviour. From Chapter Two we have seen that men are prone to all kinds of addictive behaviour. It would need a separate book to explore the different kinds of addictive behaviours responsible for some of their unhappiness. I have had to focus on just a few of the most prevalent addictions that in some way contribute to domestic violence. Women are less prone to some of these addictions but it is a growing problem for many women.

Addictive behaviour is responsible for much of the unhappiness we face, so it is right that it be part of the general awareness-raising in the process of stopping violent behaviour. Too many people and institutions, including the government, benefit hugely from our propensity for addictive behaviour. As individuals we cannot rely on anyone else to look after our best interests. We must take responsibility for our own happiness or we will continue to live miserable lives as there is always someone ready to profit from our unhappiness. Governments are also implicated in exploiting our weaknesses when they collude with big businesses that make huge profits at the expense of our health and wellbeing. Tobacco, alcohol and licit drug companies are good examples of this but not the only ones.

Perpetrators who have used violence under the influence of mind-altering substances are often looking for something, or someone else, to blame for their violence. If you have used violence when under the influence of mind-altering drugs it is as important to work on giving up the addiction. Being in touch with your real feelings is an important part of the counselling process. Mind-altering substances can have the effect of numbing or distorting real feelings and clouding judgement. It was for this reason our policy at the Everyman Centre was to work with men only after they had started counselling to stop their drug addiction. Men had to agree to not take alcohol or other mind altering substances at least eight hours before their counselling session and were discouraged from doing so straight after the session.

The worldwide use of mind-altering substances is a serious problem affecting most societies. Although drug statistics show that its use has stabilized over the last ten years, with one in every twenty people, aged 15-64 having used illicit drugs at least once in the last twelve months. Its use starts at a young age that seems to be getting younger, with hundreds of thousands of British children, some as young as 11, experimenting with hard drugs, including heroine and cocaine. Many more use cannabis, amphetamines or glue on a regular basis. There was also an increase of alcohol consumption and cigarette smoking, especially among girls.[1] That young people in such numbers turn to drugs is an issue that cannot be ignored for ever and governments need to do more to prevent abuse and help those who are already affected. Fortunately many experiment for a while and move on before any real damage is done but a sizeable minority become seriously addicted and of these some 200,000 die worldwide each year. Good news is the annual government survey of 11- to 15-year-olds shows that the rates of teenage drinking, smoking and drug use has fallen from 19 per cent to 17 per cent since 2005. Some 21 per cent had drunk alcohol in the previous week, down from 26 per cent in 2001. In the same period the proportion that has never used alcohol increased from 40 per cent to 46 per cent. The proportion who had never smoked is now 61 per cent, compared with 47 per cent when the survey was carried out in 1982.[2]

That licit drug companies are allowed to peddle their poison freely is a disgrace that can only be seen as a dereliction of duty by governments to protect its citizens from ill health, misery and early death. Research shows that some 5 million lives are claimed internationally by tobacco consumption alone and a further 2.5 million claimed by alcohol.[3] It is estimated that by 2030 some 80 per cent of the lives lost will be in the poorer countries where there is less health awareness and protection from advertising companies.[4] Not only is this failure to stem drug addiction responsible for loss of lives, it is also the cause of criminal activity and serious social problems, including domestic violence.

The reliance of governments on revenue from licit drug industries must be broken if there is to be real change; recently released papers show how a decision by the then chancellor, Harold Macmillan, not to ban tobacco was based on how revenues would be affected.[5] There may be a conflict of interest when politicians rely on big business for financial support, as highlighted by the Labour Party's fiasco over the banning of tobacco adverts. The tobacco industry benefited from the government's failure to introduce legislation on tobacco advertising on time (as promised to the electorate). When the scandal was exposed, the £1 million the Labour Party received from the tobacco industry before the elections had to be returned, leaving the government with mud on its face. Unsurprisingly that people are sceptical when the alcohol lobby wins concessions for longer opening hours, despite all the predictions by those working to alleviate the problem of alcoholism about the likely detrimental effects of this action. It is false economy for governments to rely on this type of blood money; they often have to spend much more on the social and medical problems created as a result of dependencies on these drugs, while the real benefactors walk away with huge profits, at the taxpayer's expense. Let us look at what is meant by addiction, since it is not unusual for addicts to deny their dependence.

The clinical definition is: *"an addiction is a dependence on a substance (such as alcohol) or an activity (such as gambling) even when the behaviour has become counter-productive to the health of the individual."*[6]

Addicts are often not aware that they are at risk, and it may take someone who knows them well to notice the change in their behaviour. Addiction has certain characteristic features:

- The addictive individual becomes dependent on a particular substance, behaviour or activity for the equilibrium of their body and mind.

- The absence of the substance or behaviour produces a state of physical and/or mental discomfort, known as withdrawal.

- An addict experiences powerful cravings for the substance or behaviour.

- Addiction is marked by tolerance-keeps needing more of it to feel satisfied.

- Addictive behaviour comes to dominate the individual's life in a way that is detrimental to them.

Some addictions contribute to a bad situation that can lead to domestic violence but:

*"Domestic violence can also be seen as an addiction to the power and thrill of inflicting harm and fear on others; in some individuals, violent activity raises levels of adrenaline, the arousal hormone, creating a 'rush' that can be likened to a dopamine 'high'. Individuals who are prone to violence often show deficits in impulse control which may also be shared by those who are addicted to drugs."[7]*

If you recognize the above symptoms in yourself you must seek help from a project that specializes in one of the specific areas of addiction counselling related to your addiction. If there are no places for you to obtain help then using the exercises in this chapter on a regular basis will help you with the addiction.

Let us take a closer look at some of the addictions that can and do contribute to domestic violence.

### Alcohol addiction

This is the most readily available and widely consumed drug in the world. It has a central role in social and ceremonial occasions, with some 90 per cent of the British population drinking to some degree. Addiction to alcohol generates many social problems, including violence towards women, with 44 per cent of domestic violence survivors saying their attacker was under the influence of alcohol at the time of the attack.[8] Some of the most horrific cases of domestic violence I have listened to were committed by men under the influence of alcohol.

Since the use of this drug has become widely accepted the consequences of its abuse are plain for all to see in the streets and parks of most major cities. According to a NHS study "nearly a quarter of adults are risking their health through hazardous drinking". The cost of alcoholism to the taxpayer is some £3 billion a year and alcohol is implicated in some 40,000 deaths a year in England and Wales. According to a recent report, "It is not just the binge drinkers on a Saturday nights who get into fights, crash cars and end up in the accident and emergency departments of hospitals who are the problem. The NHS is also staggering under the weight of alcohol related illness, with more than 28,000 people admitted to hospital every year because they are dependent on alcohol or have been poisoned by it". The report claims that 25 per cent of men admitted to hospital, is as a direct result of alcohol abuse.[9]

Women who drink are also in danger of doing serious damage to their health; a new study conducted into drinking and cancer has found that women who drink a glass of wine a day are more likely to develop a range of cancers. Researchers at the University of Oxford found that a daily drink significantly raised the risk of breast, liver and rectal cancer.[10]

When one considers how alcohol abuse can affect almost every part of the body it is bordering on recklessness that people continue to drink in huge numbers. Drinking alcohol puts at risk our liver, heart, digestive system, bones, skin and muscles, the brain and nervous system; add to these the risk of sexual and mental health problems, infectious diseases, malnutrition, cancer, damage to the foetus in pregnancy, anti-social behaviour, etc. If we are right-minded we would run a mile if someone offered us a drink that we were aware could affect us in these ways. It is too late for some people, as by the time they get the information they are already addicted to the taste and effect of this drug. As a matter of fact, most would strenuously defend its use, and new research shows that a majority of people in Britain do not believe they could live their lives enjoyably or successfully without alcohol.[11] So there is talk of "sensible drinking" as if such a thing is really possible - but most people are prepared to take the risk. From a survey of 1,000 people 88 per cent questioned said they would find it difficult to give up alcohol completely. Those who exploit our fondness for it are only too willing to tell us of its benefits and most of us have some myth in our heads about the health benefits of consuming alcohol. There are no clear messages from the government and often conflicting ones, so it should not surprise that we are confused most of the time about its use. Their figures show that 38 per cent of men and 16 per cent of women drink more than recommended limits, with some 1.1 million said to be dependent on alcohol and another 7.1 million seen as problem drinkers[12] - not counting you or me, of course.

The government's reliance on revenue from the alcohol industry perhaps explains some of their actions, such as the free publicity from politicians promoting its consumption, as they deliberately appeal to the working-class vote, beer or whisky glass in hand, on TV. It is suspicious when under no pressure from any group in society (except the owners of this industry) the government finds it necessary to introduce legislation for longer opening hours for drinking places, despite a survey showing that 93 per cent were opposed to this move. It is not surprising that the government has been accused of "turning a blind eye" to the problem. While other European countries are seeing a decline in the figures of those addicted, the opposite is true of Britain. Recent research shows that teenagers in Britain were the heaviest drinkers in the European Union, with schoolgirls aged 15 and 16 binge-drinking more than boys. A rethink on the government's drug policy has been urged by a report arguing for addiction to be treated as a health and social problem, not a crime issue, and that drinking and smoking should be considered as dangerous as many illegal substances.[13]

**Session Time:**
Almost all of the people I know who drink too much for their well-being deny that they have a problem. Admitting to the addiction is the first step in defeating it. Take a look at the definition again to see if you fit any of

the pointers. Getting the opinion of people who know you may be a good idea. You cannot work successfully at stopping an addiction if you do not admit to it.

Most addictions have their origin in some "hurt" that never had an opportunity to heal because no one was there to help at the time when it was installed. Taking mind-altering substances to help forget or for a feel-good factor does not solve the problem and often adds to the difficulties. Identifying the root cause of the addiction is crucial in giving it up. Only you know where that deep hurt is. Facing up to the hurt and seeking help will make it easier to beat the addiction. I am sorry for whatever happened – you did not invite or want the hurt and definitely are not to be blamed in any way for it.

> **Exercise: The roots of addiction** Take some time now to think/talk about your life to see which hurt might be the source of your addiction.

You must decide that you will not let whatever happened in the past ruin the rest of your life; you deserve better than this. The hurt is in the past, done - nothing you can do will ever change that, you can only move on. The present and the future are what are important, the past is already determined. You must move on with your life.

For some people it may be too hard to think of giving up the addiction straight away, although others have been able to do this. Cutting back on the amount of alcohol and the occasions when it is consumed is one way that has worked with some people. Think about which approach you believe will work for you and commit to using it. Admitting it is a problem and deciding to stop are the first two steps in giving up the addiction. You will have a fight on your hands, for the addiction is like a "monkey on your back" that does not want to be thrown off. Be prepared to fight as though you were fighting for your life.

Often there is a great deal of guilt attached to the addiction, which only serves to keep you locked in it. The first step is to give up any feelings of guilt. Guilt keeps you feeling bad and prevents you from taking action to remedy the situation. So with great delight in yourself, tell me about the first time you consumed alcohol. When you have finished doing this, with even more delight tell me about the things you like about alcohol. Next, I want you to make a decision to stop using alcohol: "*I decide from this moment on no more alcohol.*" Remember, you are not the addiction, it is only something that got attached to you and you can rid yourself of it. Notice the feelings that come up when you make this decision.

> **Exercise: Early memories of addiction.** Talk/think about your addiction. When did it start? What attracted you to it? What was your body's response to it?

I want you to consider the decision "*I decide from this moment on no more alcohol*" for a moment and what it means for you. I want you to decide to give up, even if just for the duration of this session. When working with clients on giving up addiction, I always keep the session light and funny. After they have made the decision I then pretend to be the addiction. I sometimes lean (as we stand) slightly against the client and keep leaning more and more heavily as they make the decision. At first they are uncomfortable with my leaning on them but do nothing. They eventually try to push me (the addiction) off as I try to stay attached to them. As they fight me off, I may start to beg and plead that they can't abandon me (the addiction, that is), I won't let them. We fool around like this for a few sessions with much laughter and sometimes tears at the end. They have opportunity to report to the group how they are progressing with giving up the addiction during the sessions. If feelings of frustration come up during this exercise remember you can always use a cushion as a punch-bag to get those feelings out. Never giving blame or reproach for how they are doing, but lots of praise for any progress has helped many perpetrators give up this addiction. You too can be helped by putting attention on giving up the addiction.

**My story: Addictions**

I had my first experience of alcohol at a young age during the Christmas season, when we were given a taste of one of the home-made brews, popular at this time of the year. We learnt to make our own wine from jamoon (a local wild fruit), but it was not until my teens that I was introduced to the taste of rum. My first part-time job, at the age of about 15, was delivering rum to the scores of "rum shops" along the East Bank of the Demerara River. For about three months I resisted my workmates' invitation to take a drink. When I did succumb to the persistent pressure and had a drink, I felt sick and vomited, swearing I would never drink again. However, the pressure "to take one" was constant and the next time I took a drink I handled it better. It was not long before I started liking the taste and effects of rum.

Around this time of experimenting with alcohol my parents separated. This broke my heart and I began to drink more regularly, to ease the pain. It did not help that I moved to the mining town of McKenzie to begin a five-year apprenticeship in the bauxite industry. There was a real drinking culture here, since there was little else to do for many of the bachelors who were also migrants. It was a macho environment and the better you were at "holding" your drink the more of a man you were considered. We often drank the whole weekend, and of course during weekdays as well. Night-shift workers usually stopped at the rum shop before going home at the end of their shift. We could get a bottle of rum anytime of the night or day and rum shops were open well before grocery shops. There was no shortage of drinking places; if you knew where to look, you could always find a place prepared to stay open all night, once you were prepared to spend. During one particularly bad spell in my early twenties I drank about a bottle of rum most nights for about a year. My drinking only eased when I met and fell in love with a student at a party. More of this story in the final chapter on relationship-building.

I knew I had a problem with alcohol when friends recounted things occurring under the influence of alcohol of which I had little or no recollection. This worried me as I could not bear to think I could have said or done something that I was not aware of, or might be ashamed of. I had noticed that my mood could be quite different under the influence. Sometimes I drank and was the most merry and friendly person; other times I was just spoiling for a fight. My worst nightmare came true when what I thought was a bad dream turned out to be reality. Under the influence I had gone to the house of an ex-lover, who was recently married, and put myself in a situation where I could rightly have been attacked. I was in no state to defend myself – never mind the embarrassment I caused.

As I remember the "dream" I had gone to Noreen's (not her real name) house during the daytime. The weather was hot and her door was slightly agar, I pushed it open and walked in, uninvited. Noreen was in bed with little on, no doubt trying to keep cool from the heat of the day. She grabbed a dress as she tried to shoo me away but I persisted in trying to grab hold of her. She no doubt realized that I was drunk as hell and decided to get out fast, making good her escape through the back door. I was right behind her as she ran into a neighbour's house.

Luckily I had worked all over the mining industry and had drunk in most bars and was known by most of the men in this small town. When the man, whose house I had entered so rudely, emerged from his bedroom, cutlass in hand I recognized him from somewhere – work or rum shop, no doubt. He probably realized straight away that I was very drunk and no real threat. I said, "Where are you going with that?" referring to the cutlass he was brandishing. At the same time I noticed a plate of food on the table, which the woman by his side had no doubt prepared for him. I was ravenous and without as much as a please, I took the plate of food from the table and began eating it, with the man and woman looking at me with disbelief, or perhaps a hint of amusement. In the meantime Noreen had made good her escape. After eating most of the man's lunch I left the house and made my way back to the main road, stopped someone I recognized with a motorcycle and demanded a lift home.

The next morning I thought, "What a crazy dream that was!" It was not until I saw Noreen about a week or two after the "dream" and she did not want to know me that it dawned on me that this had been no dream. I felt so ashamed and shuddered at the thought of what could have happened had her husband been at home at the time.

I also often endangered my life and the life of others by drinking and driving. I only stopped when I was banned for drink-driving. I had written off my wife's car after falling asleep at the wheel. It was sheer luck that no one was hurt when I swerved across the road into a common, narrowly missing a tree. After this incident I stopped drinking for three years. When I started again, I controlled how much I drank on any one occasion. Over the years I realize I can have as good a time with or without alcohol. With the help of counselling, I have almost stopped drinking altogether, choosing to drink in moderation only with special friends or on special occasions. For some people who are addicted to alcohol, complete abstinence may be the best solution.

To help break the habit it is good to keep checking on your drinking habit, I encourage you to keep a diary for this purpose. Make a decision before you go out as to how much you will drink. It may take several sessions before you are able to stick to your decision to not drink so do not give up. Making a decision not to drink at home is also a good strategy. Find a substitute drink that you like when you feel obliged to have a drink. Keep checking on how well you are able to stick to your targets. Cut down on the times of the week you drink. Avoid the situations or people who encourage you to drink too much.

**Exercise: Overcoming addiction.** Write a "counter" essay on "How I stopped my addiction". Even though you may not have given up the addiction as yet, tell me how you have achieved this goal.

### Cannabis Addiction

A small proportion of perpetrators I have worked with disclosed that they used cannabis. Most of them felt it did not contribute to their violent behaviour and some believed that the drug had a calming effect on them. I decided to include cannabis use in the awareness-raising sessions, since dependence on any mind-altering substance is not helpful in forming healthy relationships. Besides, it is not acceptable for perpetrators to attend a counselling session under the influence of any kind of mind altering substance. It is worth noting that cannabis smoking is criminalized but not tobacco smoking although it accounts for many more deaths.

Cannabis is used at least once a year by over 150 million people worldwide and is the most commonly used illegal substance in the UK. There has been much debate about its use, with many arguing for its perceived medicinal qualities; however, scientists claim that cannabis contains 50 per cent more cancer-giving agents than cigarettes. A report from the British Lung Foundation found that smoking three cannabis joints a day caused the same damage to the lining of the airways as smoking 20 cigarettes. If cannabis and tobacco are smoked together the consequences are even greater. Most cannabis smokers inhale and hold their breath for an average four times longer, resulting in more tar and carbon dioxide poisoning of the lungs.[14]

It is not only lung damage that is of concern; a recent report argues that teenagers who smoke cannabis risk future mental health illness and higher risk of depression.[15] Fortunately the popularity of this drug may be waning, with the EU drug agency reporting a decline in its use among British teenagers from 25 per cent in 2003-04 to 21 per cent in 2006-07.[16]

Giving up tobacco smoking has immediate health benefits. A study has found that five years after quitting, the risk of early death fell by 13 per cent; after 20 years of quitting there were no additional health risks.[17] Scientists have also found that to give up both smoking and drinking can stave off the onset of Alzheimer's disease. They found that drinkers develop the disease nearly five years earlier and heavy smokers about two years earlier; if we ever needed an incentive to quitting, this is it.[18]

When trying to beat an addiction it helps to replace it with a more positive habit. Smokers can, for instance, start jogging or "power walking" to counter the effect of the years of abuse of their respiratory system. Not only will you become aware of the bad effects of the addiction on your health but you will also begin some healing of the affected organs.

**Exercise: Fighting addiction.** If you are addicted to cannabis or tobacco you can beat the addiction by using the "*I decide from this moment on - no more...*" exercise, as in the section on giving up alcohol.

## Gambling

Some perpetrators were addicted to gambling and it is not hard to imagine that losing the family budget could easily contribute to feelings of low self-esteem resulting in bad behaviour. Gambling has become endemic in most countries with the "normalizing" of this addiction through the introduction of numerous national lotteries, in spite of protest from many faith-based groups in society. In Britain, playing the lottery is now an acceptable form of entertainment on prime-time television with most people gambling in one way or another.

It is not surprising that gambling is the most popular vice of young men. Research found that nine in ten have a flutter in some form, the lottery being the most likely for both men and women at 84 per cent, followed by fruit machines at 55 per cent. Horses were 45 per cent and football 21 per cent according to the survey.[19] A million people reportedly gamble online and the number of addicts keeps rising. Changes in gambling legislation could more than double the numbers of those addicted, it was claimed.[20]

Again, without lack of pressure from the electorate and deep concerns from those working with the damaging social effects of gambling, the government has introduced legislation to make it easier for the gambling industry to fleece its citizens. The new rules allow casinos, bookmakers and internet gambling firms to advertise on television, billboards and elsewhere. The bill also still allows children to gamble on "low stake, low jackpot" fruit machines, the UK being the only developed country where children can legally do so. In an attempt to counter the evidence presented on the bad effects of gambling, the conglomerates paid for their own research. This they promptly shelved when it embarrassingly came to the same conclusions as those who are opposed to gambling. Despite this, the government continues to argue that their bill will protect the vulnerable with tight regulation.

Gamblers Anonymous argue that some 375,000 people in the UK have a gambling problem and it is not unusual for some to commit suicide because of gambling debts. Many get into criminal activity to feed the addiction; some go to all kinds of extremes, such as the man who was convicted and received a two-year suspended sentence for trying to sell his kidneys to clear his gambling debts.[21]

One strategy for stopping addiction to gambling is to make a decision not to enter the betting shops that now infest our high streets or visit the online gaming websites that pester on the internet. Help is also provided by a number of organizations specializing in the different addictions and it is worthwhile seeking out what help is available.

**Exercise: Strategy for ending the addiction.** Take some time to think/talk about what you will do instead of the addiction.

Often you have had to lie to try and cover up the addiction; this is not good for your self-esteem and telling the truth will help with this. Sometimes you have had to compromise your integrity; you can work to reclaim this. There usually is some shame attached to the addiction and it is important to remember that the addiction is not you. Telling friends and family about it will be a relief to them and to you and will help beat the habit.

You have hated yourself for the addiction. This is no good for your self-esteem. Creating the conditions that make you hate yourself is unhelpful; loving yourself is important to beat any addiction. Using the exercise described in the section on alcohol but saying: "*I decide from this moment on - no more gambling*" on a regular basis will help kick this addiction.

## My story: On gambling

Because of my father's lifestyle my early years were one big gamble. Dad was a gold and diamond prospector and our livelihood depended on his luck at finding these elusive precious minerals. We enjoyed plenty when he was lucky, but mostly it was a life of hardship and disappointment. We lived every Christmas with the hope that this would be the year when we would have all the food and toys we desired. It was sad really, the number of broken promises and disappointment we had to live with. The bicycle I never received or the high-school place we could not afford I still remember.

There was a gambling culture in the village where I grew up. Older boys and men gambled under the street-lights with the roll of a dice. At weekends the "crab bush" on the river bank was the rendezvous point for gamblers. Police raids added to the excitement and the risk. My gambling addiction began at a very young age with playing "ling", a game of throwing a coin to a line marked in the ground. The thrower of the coin nearest the line is the winner, taking all the coins. As we grew up, we graduated to playing cards for money.

After leaving the village to begin my apprenticeship in the mining town, I stopped gambling for a short while before getting hooked into it again as the "yard" where I lived was at times a gambling den. There was no escape because even at work we gambled at every opportunity, especially on the night shifts. When I moved to London I stopped gambling for a few years, until I made a friend who was also a gambler on dogs and horses.

There were times I lost all or nearly all of my wages. With a young family to provide for that was irresponsibility bordering on the criminal. The one time I hit my daughter who was aged three at the time was when she was pestering me for attention as I was feeling miserable about losing money on the horses. It is easy to see how gamblers can turn nasty towards the ones closest to them when hurting.

I gambled on and off over many years but realized that most of the times I did not feel good about myself was when I had gambled – especially if I had lost. I dislike greedy people so by constantly reminding myself that greed is one of the reasons for gambling and by having counselling sessions on my gambling addiction I was able to stop completely.

> **Exercise: Breaking the habit.** What is your story of gambling? Notice any feelings as you think/talk about the ways you became addicted. Make a decision to break the habit.

### Giving up gambling

This is not easy, as the thrill of winning, with the adrenalin flow this brings, is very exciting. You would think that most gamblers would stop very easily if they experienced only loss; but research has shown that gamblers get just as excited by losing; "they are not constantly losing, they are constantly nearly winning".[22] Often gamblers also think they are hurting no one by taking risks with their money. The few successes are great encouragement that one day you will hit the jackpot. But losing your wages is no fun to the people close to you.

Feeling bad about yourself and can lead to doing bad things. Making a daily decision never to gamble and congratulating yourself at the end of the day for not succumbing is useful in helping to break the gambling habit. A good place to start is to make a decision not to enter a betting shop or gambling den and stick to it. Noticing how the odds are stacked against winning and being aware of the number of horses and dogs that are destroyed in the racing industry will also help if you have any compassion for animals. This so-called sport is really a mug's game and it is not surprising that we feel so stupid for losing. It is time to give it up.

Gamblers often are aware that they can't beat the bookie, but the addictive pull to the adrenalin flow when gambling is not easy to give up. I have seen many a man broken by this habit. Greed is what gets most people hooked on gambling; we want something for nothing. Of course, the excitement of winning also gets the adrenalin pumping. Gambling on horses and dogs or other sports is not the only problem and the trend of slot machine and scratch-card gambling is especially worrying among the young. It is calculated that the amount of losses gamblers sustain has increased from £7.5 billion to £8.5 billion between 2000 and 2005 while stakes increased from about £42 billion to £50 billion annually.[23] This might be good news for the government's coffers, as they take their pound of flesh, but it is not good for the punters.

With new legislation encouraging the proliferation of casinos, things can only get worse. Research in the USA has found that a third of casino clients are addicted and some 6 per cent of the population in the vicinity of casinos are also addicted.[24]

**Exercise: Working to end the addiction.** Think, talk or write about how different your life would be without the addictions you struggle with.

When our lives are taken over by any addiction it robs us of the energy and time to get on with our lives in a more rewarding way. Getting rid of the addiction can free up energy and time for much more rewarding pursuits such as building better relationships or taking better care of our bodies and minds. It is time to kick your addiction and move on with enjoying your life.

# CHAPTER FIVE

...........................

# PARENTING FOR CHANGE

Parenting is one of the most difficult jobs a person will ever do yet we get little preparation or support for it. We would not be expected to undertake any major expedition without map and compass, or to bake a cake for the first time without some instruction, yet for the much more complex job of parenting we find ourselves exactly in this position. The assumption that to raise a child needs no special skills is widespread and is responsible for most of the difficulties and hardships many parents face on a daily basis.

Although many parents learn by trial and error, parenting skills on the whole have improved over the generations. Some of the really bad practices prevalent not so long ago, and enshrined in proverbs such as, "children will be seen and not heard" or "spare the rod and spoil the child", are no longer widely accepted. . However the mistreatment of children is still widespread; with some three children killed every week by parents or care-givers in Britain.[1]

After listening to the stories of perpetrators about the mistreatment they endured as children I noticed that the more abusive their childhoods were the more vicious the violence they unleashed on their partners. The ones who were struck in a more controlled way tended to be more controlled about the level of violence they used. To help perpetrators "heal" from the abuse and to interrupt the patterns of violence being passed on to their children I decided on *parenting for change class*. Education or instruction alone is not enough to change deeply held patterns of behaviour; there must be some emotional content for healing to take place. We are all different and react differently to mistreatment, so individual work with perpetrators is crucial in the healing process. Perpetrators must face the mistreatment they endured as children so they can better understand their bad behaviour and begin the healing process.

Our parents did their very best in raising us and deserve no blame or disrespect even if they have not excelled as good care-givers. Many were badly mistreated themselves as children, and it should not surprise that some of this mistreatment is unconsciously passed on to their children. This is one of the ways patterns of violence transfer from one generation to the next. We can only teach what we know and, sadly, what many of us have learnt is that it is acceptable to hit children if they "misbehave". This widespread and wrongly held belief is responsible for much of the unhappiness children face and is the root cause of much of the anti-social behaviour in society.

Violence is learned behaviour that can be unlearned and parents by striving to not pass on the mistreatment they received as children can play a significant part in breaking the cycle of violence. Almost all the perpetrators I have worked with were hit as children and while it may be true that not all children who are hit grow up to be perpetrators many do. Zero-tolerance to violence is meaningless if violence towards children is tolerated. Although the behaviour of parents/caregivers can have a huge impact on violent behaviour, it would be wrong to put the blame for domestic violence on parenting skills alone. The overwhelming socialization for violence is from society as a whole. The best care-givers can do is try to protect children, especially in their formative years, from the violent socialization so prevalent. Governments can play an important role in reducing the socialization for violence if they so choose. Nelson Mandela showed the way in South Africa when he encouraged children to hand in their toy guns in exchange for a certificate signed by him.[2] In Mexico the government responded to an escalating spate of killings by drug barons and the army by banning the sale of toy guns. These are small measures but they can go a long way towards reducing the socialization for violence.

Supporting parents to raise non-violent children is absolutely necessary if we are to achieve zero-tolerance to violence. We must all get involved and there is some recognition of the demanding job of parenting in the African proverb: "it takes a village to raise a child". By contrast, some western societies regularly attack and blame parents, and especially single parents, for all the ills in society; this has to stop. Raising children in a non-oppressive environment will bring real benefits for society.

Long regarded as the "building block" of society, the model patriarchal family consisted of a man as head of the household with the wife and children somewhere beneath him. From the very beginning the patriarchal state depended on parents enforcing its norms and values. Obedience to authority is a key element in socializing children; if violence has to be used to enforce compliance, then so be it. The patriarch had full control of the family and whatever he did in the home was generally tolerated. Although most western governments no longer support the mistreatment of women in the home "reasonable chastisement" of children is still largely accepted, and in some cases positively encouraged.

Mistreating children in the family teaches them to accept oppression and is one of the key elements that has helped to support the oppressive state. This is one of the reasons why governments of whatever shade have always supported the institution of marriage and are reluctant to undermine the authority of parents, even at the expense of children's wellbeing. Successive British prime ministers of both Conservative and Labour parties have promised parents that they would never lose the right to smack children - this despite ex-prime minister Tony Blair himself admitting that hitting his children was not the best way to discipline them and that he always regretted his actions.[3]

## Healing the Hurts

Most professionals who work with parents agree that, on the whole, people tend to parent their children the way they were parented. If they had been hit and badly mistreated as children there is a pull to pass on similar mistreatment. Parents need to "heal" from their own hurtful childhood experiences if they are to interrupt the passing on of hurtful patterns of behaviour to their children. Our parents mostly hit us because they were hit themselves. When they hit they were frustrated and genuinely believed it was the right thing to do. There was no pretence in the "this will hurt me more than it does you", or the "it's because I love you" as they administered corporal punishment. You can bet that is what was done to them or worse. We often parent our children better than we were parented ourselves, with improvements especially in areas where we felt a great injustice was committed and we decide never to repeat them on our children. However, from my experience as a parent and from working with parents, I know it is not always easy to remember those decisions and to act on them, as there is a strong pull towards acting out the learnt behaviour especially when frustrated and stressed.

Acknowledging any mistreatment you received as a child and putting some attention on the hurt will help with the healing. You have to revisit some of those hurtful experiences so that you can have some feelings about them. Having a good cry is helpful, as it is part of the natural healing process of the body. Unfortunately boys are often prevented from using this process with the familiar "come on, big boys don't cry". This has left boys with a lot of unhealed hurt that manifest in the hurtful things they do as men. Girls have also had this process interrupted but perhaps not to the same extent.

**Tears:** We often confuse tears with hurting, when in fact tears ease the hurting and help with the recovery. The conditioning to suppress feelings is very heavy in many cultures. In some instances people have ended up in the mental health system for showing feelings of anger or grief. This conditioning to hide feelings must be challenged, for it is responsible for much of the unhealed hurt we carry. I encourage you to cry when hurting and to notice the difference it makes to how you feel and think afterwards. This is best done if you can have someone pay you attention at the time, since crying alone may reinforce feelings of isolation.

When hurting, it is helpful if people do not interrupt our need to cry. Such interruption happens all the time. Once while visiting a school I noticed a boy who in running tripped, hurt himself and spontaneously burst into tears. A woman quickly reaches him, takes him by the hand: "Come on, Spiderman, up you get." The crying stopped almost immediately, as he got the message that this was not what was expected of him. We have to encourage our children to show feelings when they get hurt. This interruption of the natural healing process is not only done at an early stage in our lives, it continues throughout our lives and even into old age.

I had a recent experience of this at a hospital when an ambulance arrived and a woman was rushed in on a trolley, alarm bells and red lights flashing, doctors and nurses rushing about; a real emergency. I suspected a heart attack or stroke. Shortly after the trolley was whisked away, an elderly man entered the waiting-room with a group of people. He sat down and burst into spontaneous tears. Immediately, a young woman moved to his side to try to stop him. I was sitting close to them and signalled to her with my hand and facial expression to let him be. He did cry for a bit, but they were uncomfortable with this show of feelings. Can you imagine, this was his wife of perhaps some fifty years and she could be dying, but he is not allowed to show some feelings about that?

> **Exercise: Reclaiming feeling.** What is your experience of showing tears? Stop for a moment to think/talk or write about it and allow time to have feelings.

## My story: On smacking

I don't hate my parents for the beatings I had but I am not about to proclaim that "it did me no harm", as I know it did. It made me act out my angry feelings on my siblings or other children at school. It made me feel that I was a bad child. It often terrified me and it hurt like hell.

I was hit a lot as a child and still carry a scar where my father once hit me with a leather strap. Beatings by Dad were relatively rare as he was only called in when Mom felt the punishment deserved a greater severity than she was prepared to deliver. To this day, I cannot understand why, at the age of five or six, I received one such beating that inflicted the cut from that leather strap. I recall the terror I felt as I sought refuge under a bed, with all attempts to "poke" me out with a broomstick failing to dislodge me. I remember Mom trying to stop the beating. (I pause for a moment here to feel the feelings and a let a few tears come to my eyes.) The sad thing is that I know my father loved me at least as much as my mother did.

At one period in my life it felt as if my two older brothers and I had regular beatings almost weekly. In our search for adventure and excitement, we wandered from home for hours. My mom was terrified that we would come to harm and sometimes with good reason. We were always doing risky things, but the one she feared the most was our swimming. For us, it was the most fun thing we did. There were no playgrounds and swings and things like that where we grew up. If we were not swimming in the trenches that surrounded the sugarcane fields, we were swimming in the Demerara River (this is where the name of the brown sugar you use comes from). Weekends when we left home in the mornings we were never in a hurry to return, high tide and low tide would come and go as we swam or played on the river-bank. We figured we were going to get "licks" anyway, so we might as well enjoy ourselves as much as possible. School holidays must have been a nightmare for mom and it was the time of the most beatings; sometimes mom hid our pants so we could not leave the house.

During one of the beatings I made a decision never to hit my children if I became a father. I was standing in line waiting my turn, for the beatings usually began with my eldest brother. This is where the writing gets hard for me. (I stop to cry for a while.) I probably got the least lashes, as my mother must have been a bit tired by the time she got to me, the youngest of the three. The beatings stopped when my eldest brother, aged about 14 at the time, just stood there and absorbed the lashes without moving a muscle. Mom got frustrated, threw away the strap and declared that it was down to my father from then on. The beatings almost ceased since Dad was mostly away and anyway did not have the same fears about our safety, being much more relaxed about us taking risks. It is a real shame that we had to endure so much pain and resentment. My parents probably felt really bad about themselves as well. Yet there was nothing unusual in this as all our friends had similar experiences.

> **Exercise: Early memories.** What are your memories of being hit as a child? Remember, this is not about blaming, but so that you can notice how some of the patterns for violence were installed, and to allow healing to take place. Take time to notice any feelings that come up.

Getting to the root cause of domestic violence often means taking perpetrators back to childhood experiences. The stories may be quite painful, as this is where the patterns for mistreatment get laid in. Because of the need to feel loved by our care-givers it is sometimes hard to accept that our parents/carers would mistreat us in any way unless we "deserved" it. We are so desperate for this "love" from our parents/carers that we are prepared to believe it is because they care for us that they mistreat us. Some parents/carers really believe this and have said, at the time of the mistreatment that "it is for your own good" and would somehow make you a better person. It should not surprise that many perpetrators say they hit their partners "because he/she deserved it". I have sometimes been attacked for making "excuses" for perpetrators when I air this viewpoint. The reality is most perpetrators initially deny that the mistreatment they received had anything to do with their violent behaviour. They are more likely to blame the other person for "pushing them" too far. Being in denial is not useful when trying to change attitude and behaviour. It takes a little time and patience for perpetrators to begin to understand how their childhood experiences could have something to do with their violence. If you justify the violence done to you there is a good chance you will try to justify the violence you perpetrate on your partner.

**Violence during pregnancy:**

This is one of the hardest aspects of domestic violence for me to write about. It really hurts and shames me that men can be violent to their pregnant partners. It hurts me even to think about it. I have had to stop for a moment to weep before being able to carry on writing, knowing that "Very often the abdomen becomes the focus of physical assaults during pregnancy, and some babies are miscarried, stillborn or born disabled as a result."[4]

These are not isolated attacks a survey of patients by Professor Gene Feder showed that four in 10 women in Hackney, London, suffered domestic violence with 15 per cent being attacked while they were expecting a child. A quarter of the women said the violence was worse than when they weren't expecting.[5]

If you have been violent to your partner during pregnancy you will need some extra support to get over this type of abusive behaviour and it would be good for you to seek some face-to-face support to do this. If this is not possible you will have to go back to your early memories to understand where this viscous, abusive behaviour is coming from. Maybe you saw your father or some other male abuse a pregnant woman in your childhood and you were unable to prevent it. Maybe violence was done to you in the womb and you are acting out this distress in an unconscious attempt to get help for yourself. Maybe you resent the pregnancy and are using this very vulnerable time for a woman to impose your total control. Whatever the cause of this callous act, you must make a decision that this never happens again. Try using the following commitment daily:

> *I solemnly promise that I will cherish all my children, however small, and will do everything in my power to always protect them from harm, from this moment on. And this means I will never again hurt a woman.*

**Exercise: Healing the hurts.** What is your earliest memory of being hit? Think/talk about it and allow for feelings.

Parenting for change can have a huge impact on ending domestic violence. Deciding to raise children who abhor violence can make a huge difference to the society we live in. We can start by making changes in the following three areas:

## 1.Smacking

All the perpetrators I have worked with who have used physical violence were hit as children. I noticed that those who had been badly beaten were more likely to use greater physical violence than those who were hit less severely as children. It usually takes perpetrators a few sessions to remember what it really was like. One man told me what a "brilliant" childhood he had growing up in the Caribbean. About five minutes later, he was describing how his father "picked a whip from a tree" and beat him for riding a pig. This seemed reasonable to him, as his father had "warned him many times". His "brilliant" childhood, it transpired, was by comparison with what he saw happening to other children around him. It should not surprise that most of his violence to his partner was because she did not "do as she was told."

Many of us will have experienced being hit as children. A recent UN report shows that "violence to children is widely accepted as normal around the world", with at least 106 countries allowing physical punishment in schools and 147 countries having not outlawed the punishment of children.[6] Also research in Britain and the USA shows that 52 per cent of one-year-old children are hit at least once a week by their parents. Three-quarters of parents smack their babies in the first year of life, mostly as a result of irritation or anger.[7] Infants under twelve months are more likely to be victims of homicide than the rest of the population: three children a week die in the UK at the hands of their parents/carers and often no convictions are obtained against the murders.[8]

It is likely that most people who advocate the hitting of children as an acceptable form of discipline have themselves been hit as children. Many people argue that the "little smacks" they received did them no harm. It is not unusual to see a child who has been smacked shrug it off in an act of defiance - "didn't hurt" - determined not to give the smacker the satisfaction of thinking they hurt them. Whether or not it hurt physically, what is certain is that they are sure to have felt it emotionally. Some people have closed minds on the subject and will defend this right to hit children no matter what arguments or evidence are put before them. To the people declaring that the smacks they received did them no harm, I say: "But that is the harm it has done." They hit children or have become advocates of hitting children, thereby perpetuating the use of violence that often results in domestic and other forms of violence.

Parents need to know that there are real benefits from not hitting children. Professor Murray A. Straus, who has researched the effects of violence on children for over 35 years, argues that parents who do not hit their children instead reason with and explain to them more. This process is beneficial for the child in that it helps their cognitive development. They have to use their brains more; as a result their intelligence develops more rapidly, as compared to children who are hit. Straus argues that the benefits are not limited to enhanced mental ability; "the other three studies I reviewed show that ending corporal punishment is likely to also reduce juvenile violence and other crime."[9]

Over the years I have worked with men with violent behaviour patterns, I have seen only one man who had never been hit as a child.

When he had arguments with his partner and felt frustrated and angry, he would sometimes hurt himself by punching his legs or banging his head against a wall. As we delved into his childhood experiences, it transpired that his punishment for bad behaviour was to be sent to his room. Left there for too long, he would take out his bad feelings on himself. As a result he learnt to hurt himself when he was angry or frustrated. Perpetrators who use emotional or psychological violence have often been abused in this way as young ones. The exercises to overcome violent behaviour will also help perpetrators of psychological and emotional abuse.

### 2. Interrupting the socialization for violence

Many of the men I have worked with saw their fathers or other men being violent to their mothers. One perpetrator I worked with frequently saw his father hitting his mother and when she left them because of the violence his father then had a succession of relationships, all of which were violent. He recollected one woman being thrown down the stairs naked. This kind of exposure to violence is bound to distress anyone witnessing it and without support to get over the bad effects there is a good chance they will act out this distress later on in their lives.

According to a UN report, up to 275 million children witness domestic violence annually.[10] This has serious consequences for society as studies show that one of the key factors for perpetrators is them having witnessed domestic violence as children.[11] Other research has shown that nine out of ten children living with domestic violence were in the same or an adjacent room when the abuse has taken place.[12] But witnessing domestic violence or being hit themselves are not the only factors; as we have seen in the chapter on men, there is additional socialization for violence for boys especially, from peers and other sources:

## Screen violence

Television, videos and video games play a major role in the socialization for violence. Albert Bandura and his associates have demonstrated that simply watching violence on television can increase the aggressive behaviour of young children. The basic experiment was to show an adult hitting about a life-sized doll, with a show of physical aggression followed with verbal abuse. They then allowed the children to play with the doll. Not only did the children repeat the adult's behaviour, they also made up some of their own aggressive behaviour.[13]

George Gerbner and his associates have studied violence for over twenty-five years. They studied prime-time and Saturday morning television and found that "violence prevails in eight out of ten programmes." Violence occurs six times each hour. With cartoons it was worse, about eighteen acts of aggression every hour.[14] Just imagine: our children watch more violence than we do, yet we are surprised when they act out what they are subjected to on a regular basis. As to be expected, the network TV companies deny any connection with children's violent behaviour, because it was "only cartoons". But research has shown that viewing cartoons "induces kids to wallop each other as well".[15] Children learn from the things they see and experience around them; this is why nurseries have long discouraged the use of toy weapons on their premises. Yet the Labour government can give the go-ahead for toy guns in nurseries with the excuse that "Creating situations so that boys' interests in these forms of play can be fostered through healthy and safe risk-taking will enhance every aspect of their learning."[16] This, at a time when we have an explosion of street crime involving knives and guns, can only be considered recklessness at the very least.

In the USA, a four-year-old after a fight took his mother's loaded gun from a handbag and shot his sibling, aged two, in the head. Another boy aged five stabbed his ten-year-old sister in the neck with a kitchen knife over an argument about a games console. How many stories of this kind will we have to read about before action is taken about the levels of violence our children experience?

There are various experiments linking television viewing to aggressive behaviour. A longitudinal study by Leonard Eron and Rowell Huesmann found a "high correlation between watching violence on television and aggressive behaviour" among eight-year-old boys. Eleven years after the initial study, 211 of the boys were restudied. Those nineteen-year-olds who had watched a lot of TV violence at age eight were found to be more aggressive than those who had not. But this is not the only damage done; it was also shown that watching violence on TV desensitizes children to acts of violence and hardens them to the feelings of those who are the targets of aggression, making it easier for them to commit acts of violence themselves.[17]

It is not only children who are affected by screen violence as other researchers have shown that TV violence also affects adults. Recently a headless, handless and nearly nude body was discovered in Los Angeles. Two brothers, aged 15 and 20, were charged with the murder of their mother. The investigators believe the 41-year-old woman was strangled in her bed. One brother reportedly confessed to the murder, telling detectives that he and his half-brother dismembered the body after seeing it done by characters on "The Sopranos".[18]

Violent video games are increasingly in the dock. Research by Dr Craig Anderson and Professor Karen Dill into video games conducted a study of 227 college students about their aggressive attitudes. They found "that students who reported playing more violent video games in junior and high school engaged in more aggressive behaviour." Their research was published a year after the Columbine high-school massacre in which 12 students and a teacher were killed and 23 wounded. The boys had previously made a classroom video of the scene they re-enacted for a project and left a recording describing "how the slaughter would be just like their favourite video game, Doom", a video game licensed by the US army to train soldiers to kill.[19] Despite this evidence the production company continues to churn out more of the same with the release of Doom 3, featuring "decapitations, exploding heads and stomachs, and an array of terrible weapons, including axes, chainsaws and rocket launchers." Another video game, Manhunt, was also in the dock after the parents of a murdered 14-year-old said it influenced his 17-year-old killer. The killing of 2-year-old James Bulger shocked the world when two 10-year-olds were convicted of his killing. They had been addicted to watching the video Child's Play 3, which had similar scenes to the crime they committed.

But it is not only violent video games that cause concern. Doctors complain that US children are subjected to 8,000 killings and 100,000 other acts of violence on TV before the age of 12. "Media violence is bad because it affects young children. Violence is learned behaviour," Dr Robert McAfee reminds us.[20] In Britain a Daily Mail study showed that TV networks in a typical week show some 400 killings, 119 woundings and 27 sex attacks.[21]

The big screen is also in the dock: "Mainstream movies are getting darker and more violent. As Quentin Tarantino's recent film project, Grindhouse, demonstrates, the worst of the violence is often directed at women."[22] A teenager nicknamed Slasher, with 20 convictions to his name and recently jailed for life for stabbing a woman jogger, was described as the UK's "most violent youth". One neighbour reportedly said that the youth's heroes were Al Capone and Tony Montana (Al Pacino's drugs boss character) in the film Scarface, which he watched repeatedly.[23] French detectives say the couple who killed four people in Paris may have been influenced by the movie *Natural Born Killers*.[24] The film was linked to ten deaths with one fourteen-year-old decapitating a girl of 13 after telling friends he wanted to kill someone and become "famous, like the natural-born killers".[25] In England three teenage boys were alleged to have copied the film *Reservoir Dogs* in their killing of another teenager.[26] More recently "The Campus Killer" re-enacted scenes in a video he made based on a violent South Korean film, before he massacred 32 students and teachers in a school in Virginia, USA.[27]

### 3. Control

Controlling behaviour is a major contributory factor in domestic violence. One perpetrator I worked with who was able to stop his violent behaviour had great difficulty maintaining a relationship because of his controlling behaviour. Women found his possessiveness attractive in the first instance, but it soon became too much for them as he tried to have complete control of their lives. When I explored this aspect of his behaviour it became clear that his dad was a control freak who also abused. As children, they were not allowed to have their own thoughts and opinions, they were always wrong, he was always right. They had to carry out his wishes exactly, or be punished, often in a most brutal fashion.

Most perpetrators have some element of this controlling behaviour. The "reasons" I hear them give for their violence are usually about control - that he/she came home late, did not prepare tea on time, was argumentative, wore the wrong clothes, had the wrong friends, and so on. Controlling patterns are very prevalent. If you think about it, you can see that most adults spend a lot of time trying to control children. Children get told what to wear, how to sit, when to sleep or wake, when to stop, when to go; I even heard a man tell a child not to sneeze.

On top of this, children are often treated as insignificant, their wishes rarely solicited or taken into account. Children get picked up and put down at will. They are treated as though they have no choice and many grow up believing they have none. Children who don't co-operate with adults' wishes face disapproval, if not violence. It is not surprising that many adults fail to see that they do have choice. Most perpetrators think they had no choice but to hit their partners.

The reality is you do have choice. You could have walked away, run, cried, asked for help sat on your hands whatever-but you did not have to hit-that was the choice you made however much it was influenced by your own past exposure to mistreatment. A first step is ending the controlling behaviour. This is learnt behaviour that can be unlearnt by noticing how the patterns were installed in the first place. Making a decision to change, and frequently working at stopping the behaviour will make a big difference to your life.

> **Exercise: Unlearning control patterns.** What was it like for you? Take some time to think/talk or write about the way you were controlled as a child and allow time for feelings.

**My story: As parent**
Although I made a promise that I would never hit my children I found myself doing exactly that at times. One incident with my eldest son reminded me of the promise I had made, so I called my children together and apologized for the times I had hit them and promised it would end. This was harder than I expected, as when I was really stressed or frustrated,

I would forget my promise; but I was committed to not hitting them and never gave up on my attempts to stop and eventually did. I was doing a lot of parenting at the time in an enforced "role reversal" with my wife, as she resentfully went out to work and I reluctantly started minding home. I was surprised to find that after a short while adjusting to the change I really began to enjoy being a "house husband".

I had spent most of my childhood out of doors and wanted the same for my children. It was also more fun and less stressful spending time with them outdoors. In the summer I made kites for us to fly; we would pack a lunch basket and spend much of the school holidays in parks. There wasn't an adventure playground we were not familiar with for miles around. During this period, on the estate where we lived I was stopped by a pensioner, who said to me, "What a fine example of a father you are." I doubt I will ever be paid a compliment that will mean more to me.

During this period of unemployment I was still gambling and on one occasion lost all of the money I had on the horses. I was sitting in my chair feeling sorry for myself and cursing my luck. What was I going to tell my wife when she returned from work? My daughter was trying to get my attention as I sat there, deflated and mad at myself. I reacted to her tugging at my arm for attention by smacking her on the leg.

If I had any doubts about the wrongness of hitting children, this experience was enough to dispel them. My daughter had never been hit before this and she reacted immediately. Tears gushed from her eyes as she said, in the most shocked and astonished voice I have ever heard from her: "How dare you? How dare you smack me, Daddy?" I shall always remember that. She knew that I had no right to hit her. The indignation she showed me left me in no doubt that it should ever happen again. I ignored all the psychological wisdom, about not punishing and showing affection to children shortly after, and immediately hugged her and apologized with tears rolling down my checks (as they do now). Hitting children can never be right.

**Case study 2:**

I started working with Arthur when he wrote to the Everyman Centre asking for help. He was coming to the end of a long prison sentence for manslaughter and this was to be part of his preparation for release into the community. He was aged 45 at the time and the father of nine children. At this stage he had spent half of his life in prison for violent crimes, including armed robbery and grievous bodily harm. Although most of his violent offences were committed against men, some women were also injured.

Arthur was born in the Caribbean and lived with his dad after his mom moved to London. His dad was a preacher and strict disciplinarian who frequently beat him, after one particular vicious beating, Arthur at the age of thirteen, ran away from home. He had been tied to a tree, which had a red ant nest at the base of the trunk, in the midday sun and beaten with an electric cord until he feinted. His crime? Kissing the neighbour's daughter! They were both aged about twelve. His mother sent for him a year later to live with her in London. When Arthur started schooling his mother was called to the school and questioned by the police about the scars on his back. The teacher had noticed the scars inflicted by the beatings from his father when he was changing for physical education.

Arthur had stabbed quite a few men in his time. As he recounted it, whenever he got into an argument with a man and he could hear the tension in their voice escalating he would decide to "get in there first". He always knew from his father's voice when he was about to get a beating. The person he really "wanted to kill" was his father, and he was disappointed that he had been cheated of this by his father's death in the Caribbean.

Working on his childhood experiences of violence, over several months in individual and group-work sessions, he recounted some of the numerous beatings by his father. Once Arthur recognized where his anger and violence was coming from he could begin to "heal" from the mistreatment. Recognizing what triggered his violence has helped him to "block" the trigger from operating, if there was danger in an argument.

I worried that Arthur would get into fights, as he would not break away from his community, where he has a reputation for violence and danger always lurked. One night he got involved in a fight when he intervened as a peacemaker and someone hit him on the head with a bottle, requiring him to have stitches. Everyone was amazed that his assailant was still alive. Arthur was proud that he could now walk away from a fight. He was determined that his life will never be the same again and his violent past was behind him. He is now happily married and recently reminded me that this was the longest stretch in his adult life that he had not been in prison - about fifteen years now.

## Fathers

Professor Charlie Lewis of Lancaster University spent twenty years researching the effects of fathers on parenting and came to the conclusion that fathers do matter. He suggests that fathers could be as important as mothers in shaping children's futures. Children who were close to their fathers were more likely to do well at school, stay out of trouble and have a large circle of friends. At six months, babies with actively involved fathers score higher in tests of physical and mental development. It is not only babies who benefit as men who spend a lot of time in charge of their children are more confident and satisfied as fathers.[28]

Fathers, with an enlightened approach to parenting can make a huge difference to the kind of society we want. We can access much more information about raising young children than our parents ever did. In the past 30 years we have learned a lot more about what children know and how they learn. For centuries psychologists and philosophers thought that babies were the opposite of adults. They were thought of as emotional and passive, incapable of rational thought. The popular myth of baby's mind as a blank slate, waiting for us to write the script for them, is no longer valid. Alison Gopnik *et al.* argue in *How Babies Think* that scientists have only recently begun to appreciate just how much babies know, and how much and how quickly they learn. They see three new elements to this new picture. First, children know a great deal, literally from the moment they are born. Secondly, they are born with extremely powerful learning abilities, more powerful than the most sophisticated computer. And, finally, grown-ups appear to be "programmed" unconsciously to teach babies and young children just the things they need to know.[29]

## Mothers

The first relationship the child has is with mother, most of the early days, weeks, months and years are mostly spent with mother. These are some of the most important years in a child's life. Mothers are in an ideal position to influence the child's development. There are many distractions but her influence for a short period will be the most decisive. With a little bit of support and information mothers can make a real difference to the shape of the world. Children do not forget those early years, which psychologists are agreed are the most important for the human. Parenting for change would be to treat little ones with love and respect and to not hit or mistreat them in any way. Sadly mothers' influence starts to wane as peers, TV and the culture in which the child is raised becomes more significant in determining the child's behaviour and attitude. The socialization for violence is so overwhelming that it is hard for even the most vigilant mother to protect their children from it.

## Absent Fathers

Research shows that many fathers lose all contact with their children when there is a breakdown in a relationship. This is really sad, as children desperately need fathers in their lives; but they want them in good shape. Children need to know that they are loved and wanted and will not be used as an emotional football between fighting parents. Whatever the difficulties you must take responsibility for sorting it out. This may mean taking time to get yourself in good emotional shape so that you can deal with the break-up, however difficult that may be for you. If there has been violence you must be sure that you will no longer use violence before trying to get back into their lives. There is no point being in a child's life if you will cause unnecessary distress to the child and mother.

You have to clean up your act for the child/children's sake. I have worked with so many clients who were deeply unhappy because their fathers were not there for them when they needed them. If your own dad was not there for you this is probably the biggest factor in your absence, but you must not let it hold you back from getting close to your children. No matter how much time has passed they will want a relationship with you, make no mistake.

Examine your motives for the contact, to ensure that it is not about making life difficult for the mother. You must heal whatever hurt caused the separation before you can have a relationship that would be good for you and for the children.

## Case study 3:

John had finished the individual sessions and was doing group work. In the class on parenting for change he realized that he was behaving in the same way as his father had done.

John's father regularly drank on a Saturday then returned home from the pub and soon found an excuse to abuse them. His father had been a military man, who showed little affection and was very authoritative. He had a habit of "storing" up punishment for any misdemeanours over the week. However much they tried to "be good" he was sure to get them on the state of their shoes; which they could never polish to meet his standards.

During sessions John realized that he was doing the same thing to his children, without consciously being aware of it. The realization was surprising and enlightening for him. He talked about the mistreatment and sobbed for the way he was mistreated by his father, and made a commitment to change his behaviour. Most of his violence to his wife occurred as she tried to intervene whenever he began hitting the children.

We worked out a strategy for him to spend more time with the children on Saturdays so he had less visits to the pub. After a few weeks of interrupting the pattern of abusive behaviour I could see the real joy returning to John's face as he described his changed relationship with his wife and children. "I think they like me," he reported to the group and was really pleased that he was now having a happy relationship with them.

## Special time for children

Children value the time parents spend with them, if that time is well spent; it is one way of letting them know that you care. Let them choose an activity and do it with. Giving them control over what to do, and how, is in great contradiction to the control usually exercised in their lives. It will also help you give up any controlling patterns of behaviour you may have.

You can start this exercise by setting aside a time when you will do this "special time" with your child. It is good to set the specific time when the special time begins and ends and you must communicate this to the child. It is a period that will require a special effort on your part to follow the lead of the child and may require a great deal of patience on your part. They may want to take this time to do the things they are normally not permitted to do. If they have not for instance been permitted sweets they may well want to binge at the sweet shop. Or they may want to take the lead in doing things in the park with you following their lead. You have to remain delighted in them whatever the activity they choose to do in this time. You will notice their confidence and happiness increase. As you do it more and more you will find that you are able to extend the special time for longer periods. Remember this is also beneficial for you in unlearning your control patterns of behaviour.

Children look to us as role models; the way we behave as adults is extremely important for the young minds around us. What we do and say, how we behave will influence them. If children are treated well and not exposed to violence they are unlikely to grow up to hurt anyone. If girls are treated with respect and shown love by their parents they would never put up with an abusive relationship for any length of time. Children whose parents take care to show that they respect their thinking and wishes will come to expect this in their relationships. In my experience of working with perpetrators I have noticed that women, who have not been mistreated by their parents as girls, do not tolerate domestic violence for any length of time.

Parents have a great deal of power as a force for change. Think what would happen if all parents raised children who have never been mistreated or exposed to violence acts? If parents also refused to give toys and idols of violence we would have started to really change society. Just imagine what would happen if boys all over the world refused to fight in times of war-mongering. Our leaders would have to find other ways of settling disputes that do not force us to kill or be killed - they already do this when it suits them. As parents we can make a real difference; let us take up the challenge of "zero tolerance" to violence and know that it is in our power to change the world.

# CHAPTER SIX

.............................

# BUILDING LOVING RELATIONSHIPS

Most of the men I have worked with declared undying love for the women they hurt. Some even attempted suicide because they felt so bad about hurting their partner. Although this can be interpreted as manipulation - another way to make partners feel bad about themselves or an attempt to gain sympathy for bad behaviour - it also shows how confused perpetrators are about what loving means. But it is not only the men who are confused about expressions of love as I have heard women defend the men who abused them with the reasoning that his abuse was proof that he loved them. This sentiment I have heard expressed in several parts of the world. It is clear to me that the mistreatment children received followed by expressions of love has left many confused about what loving is about. How else can we explain that some women believe it is because the man loves them that he will abuse them?

I got the idea for "love class" for my programme with perpetrators when I picked up a little red book in a second-hand bookshop. The title was simply *Love*. The author, Leo Buscaglia, believed that love is a learned phenomenon; we all have the potential to love but we have to develop this potential, or it will not happen. He believed it is never too late to learn to love because we have this potential and never lose it. He argued that love could modify behaviour. This struck me as being true and fitted my experience of loving, so I decided to incorporate *love class* into my programme with perpetrators.

Buscaglia believed that it was impossible or unnecessary to define love since it means different things to different people. It is an emotion, but "it is also a *response* to an emotion therefore an *active* expression of what is felt. Love is not learned by osmosis. It is actually acted out and acted upon."[1] If the people around us are not demonstrative of loving we will hardly learn what loving is about. He quotes from the Bible (I Corinthians, 13):

> Love is patient and kind; love is not jealous, or conceited, or proud; love is not ill-mannered, or selfish, or irritable; love does not keep a record of wrongs: love is not happy with evil, but is happy with the truth. Love never gives up: its faith, hope and patience never fail. Love is eternal.... There are faith, hope and love, these three; but the greatest of these is love.

In her book *All About Love*, bell hooks asserts that it is important to have love defined and she is grateful for the definition of love "as the will to extend one's self for the purpose of nurturing one's own or another's spiritual growth" from *The Road Less Travelled* by M. Scott Peck. She believes that "when we understand love as the will to nurture our own and another's spiritual growth, it becomes clear that we cannot claim to love if we are hurtful and abusive. Love and abuse cannot coexist."[2] Having a definition, bell hooks argues, gives us a yardstick by which to measure ourselves. It is a useful reference point to which we need address ourselves regularly. There should be no confusion by what loving is.

The truly loving person does not hurt anyone or thing and this is especially true of self. Most perpetrators I have worked with were badly mistreated as children and rarely experienced what real love is about. They did not have love in the first place so how can they give it? But all is not lost and I agree with Buscaglia they have the potential but it has to be developed. Having a definition as bell hooks asserts will help keep the focus on what is to be achieved.

Many of us did not grow up with good models of loving; we mistake possessiveness, jealousy, insecurity and sometimes mistreatment as expressions of love. As bell hooks states: "Most of us find it difficult to accept a definition of love that says we are never loved in a context where there is abuse." Because of a need to feel loved by those who parent us we often excuse their bad behaviour, blame ourselves for any mistreatment and internalize the notion "that love can coexist with abuse. And in extreme cases that abuse is an expression of love."[3]

Fortunately it is never too late to unlearn this misinformation. "To begin by always thinking of love as an action rather than a feeling is one way in which anyone using the word in this manner automatically assumes accountability and responsibility."[4] Using Peck's definition of love to compare with what you have been doing in your relationships in the name of love, you begin to see where you have gone wrong and can begin to figure out how to fix it.

Taking responsibility for changing your behaviour is easier if you are aware of the oppressive ways (often in the name of culture or custom) in which you behave. By taking action to unlearn the oppressive behaviour you have incorporated, you begin to liberate yourself. You are not inherently oppressive and the patterns of bad behaviour you have learnt and claim as "the way I am" can be unlearnt with a determination and commitment to change.

Many of the perpetrators I have worked with were men who have tried to control their partners in every way; telling them how to dress, who they can have as friends, when and where they can go, even what to think. This is very limiting for anyone and is not what love is about. This is about stifling love. If we truly love someone we want to see them grow, to flower into the best human possible. Love does not try to limit, but provides wings so that loved ones can soar, without limits to their flying. Striving to possess someone will not encourage this growing. If you view your partner as a possession you are bound to feel responsible for their every action, that what they think or do reflects on you. This is a huge burden to carry and you need to free yourself of it right now. You will not have a moment's peace if you try to control another's mind. It is not acceptable; although they may do as you wish out of fear, they will never respect or love you for this. In my experience, extreme possessiveness is one of the most significant indicators of domestic violence.

**Exercise: Relationship-building.** Which behaviours have caused difficulty for your relationship? Think/talk or write about what you need to do to change them.

### Love as behaviour modifier

Buscaglia was able to secure financial support for his "love class" at his university by devising the above title for his class. His argument was that the power of love could change behaviour and he used this thesis to justify teaching the class. I believe that if we truly love someone and they were not happy about some of our behaviour we would do our best to change it even if just to please them. If you really love your partner as you say you do you would find it in you to stop your violence. I have experienced the power of love to change. Had it not being for my falling in love I would probably not have changed my drinking habits and lifestyle at the time

I did. As mentioned in the chapter on addictions, I was drinking far too much on a regular basis in my late teens and early twenties when I met this high-school student at a party. Falling in love with her helped me to stop drinking and return to studying, passing my exams and setting myself on a new path.

**Love Class.**

A lot of safety and closeness will have been established by the time we got to this stage in the group-work process. I usually hugged the men in the individual sessions when they arrived and also when they finished the session. From the first group-work session the men would have been encouraged to hug each other and would have learnt from the individual sessions the importance of expressing feelings. Before long we have a really safe group, with men not being embarrassed to show their feelings. I encouraged the men to get at least four hugs a day and many reported that it makes a real difference to how they feel about themselves.

A regular feature of the class was to have the men talk about their experiences of falling in love. Sadly, not all had stories to tell but it was usually a fun time, revealing how strangely men can behave when in love. I would participate in this exercise, sometimes telling about the time I fell in love with a woman who was a political activist and artist. I had seen her perform her poetry and heard her songs and "fell" in love with her from that moment. We lived in the same area and we accidentally met in the street one day. She complained about the decorator who was working on her flat at the time so I offered my services. As I started the job we got into lots of political discussions over the days and I could feel myself falling more and more in love, sleepless nights and all. I could bear it no longer and decided to tell her of my feelings one morning. She did not respond straight away and I was just relieved to get it off my chest. She had to go to work that day but not before leaving a loving note. I was completely over the moon and during my lunch break as I sat in the café with my fish and chips in front of me sprinkling the condiments a woman interrupted me by saying: "Mister, that is the sugar." Probably I would have eaten it without noticing the difference at all!

> **Exercise: Early memories.** Write or talk about your experience of falling in love?

## Healing the hurts

If you have been neglected or mistreated in any way as a child it is important to acknowledge that hurt, put some time into "healing" from the hurt and move on. There is not much you can do about the past hurt; it has happened you cannot change that. You can only look to the future. You have all the rest of your life before you. To let a hurt (that happened at a time when you did not have the power to stop it) affect the rest of your life is to give in to the abuse. You were not to blame for the abuse. It was *their* distress not yours, as usually the abuser was acting out something that was done to them. You were always innocent. You must not allow the distressing experience to rob you of the possibility of living a happy life.

Remembering your goodness is important in the recovery process. You came into this world inherently good and any of the bad things you do is a result of the mistreatment and misinformation you experienced as a little one. Reclaiming your goodness is important if you are to stop your violent behaviour. To recover from mistreatment you must go back to that little boy/girl to reclaim him/her. You have to do this. You have to heal from whatever hurts has led to you doing hurtful things. Only you will know what that hurt is and I encourage you to face it. Remember people who really love and respect themselves would never hurt anyone.

I encourage you to think about the things that really made you feel special and to go after them. The effect of mistreatment is that we feel bad about ourselves. You have to let go of this. You are an inherently good, intelligent, lovable, creative, co-operative loving human being. Any other attitude you hold of yourself is just sheer distress. Use the affirmations given above regularly and notice the difference to your life in a short space of time.

> **Exercise: On loving.** Think about what hurt you need to "heal" from in order to really start loving. Talk or write about it and allow time for feelings.

Our relationships with other humans are not easy at the best of times and we have no choice but to try and manage those relationships as best we can. With a little information and support for managing relationships we could do a lot better. We are continually striving to be better humans and even those children raised by the most damaged adults around them will strive to be better than their caregivers. This approach has helped me stay positive in my work with perpetrators of domestic violence. If people have not been mistreated, neglected and hurt in some way in the first place they would not harm others.

One of the characteristics of humans is our gregarious nature: we thrive from being in each other's company. We need one another to realize our full potential as humans. We only have to notice what happens to children who were raised by animals, "feral children" as they are known, to be convinced that we need each other to be truly human. We develop as good, well-adjusted people if we have good well-adjusted humans around us. All too often the adults around us have been damaged by their childhood experiences and some of this mistreatment they pass on unwittingly to their children.

A feature of the loving relationship is equality; but from the inception of modern states women and children were considered by patriarchy to be "lesser than" ¬ not exactly the way to go about building a society based on love and respect. Men have internalized many aspects of the oppression inherent in such a union, and often behave in oppressive ways to their partners and children. Men have been encouraged to believe that they have power over women and have grown to expect services, including sexual, from women as of right. This was enforced in law and not too long ago in the UK it was legal for a man to rape his wife in marriage and it is still legal for men to do so in many countries today.

Women also have internalized many aspects of the oppression, acting as though they are "lesser than" in the relationship. The socialization is that a "good" wife is one who obeys and serves her husband and it is not uncommon for women to go hungry while they feed their husband and children in times of hardship. We must confront and break these oppressive patterns of behaviour if we are to achieve equality.

**Self-love:** To be able to give love you must first have it; if you do not have love for yourself you cannot give love to anyone. Cultivating love for self is crucial in defeating domestic violence as many of the perpetrators I have worked with could not remember being loved as young ones. The truth is most of us were loved as babies, even if for a moment. If you suffered a lot of mistreatment as a child it is good to imagine that you were welcomed to the world, loved and then the adults forgot to keep showing that love. Yes, you were loved, even if only for a moment and it is enough. That memory is buried deep inside somewhere, if only you can get to it. Cultivating loving ways is not so difficult and making a "decision" to do so is the first step in recovery. Using affirmations on a daily basis is useful in this; try **"I decide from this moment on to love myself completely"** and this means never hurting anyone, eating well, etc.

It is important to have love for self. People who believe themselves to be "shits" do shitty things. It has been shown that people with low self-esteem do not find it hard to commit immoral acts, since committing immoral acts is not dissonant with their self-concept. On the other hand people with high self-esteem are more likely to resist the temptation to commit immoral acts, because to behave immorally would produce a great deal of dissonance.

Remembering the times you felt loved will contradict feelings of lovelessness. Often the pull is to remember only bad experiences but with patience you can also recall the good times.

## My story: Loving self

One of the acts of loving I felt from my mother was her caring about our appearance generally she took care of our nails, hair and skin she also did wonders to put tasty food on the table and made our living conditions as comfortable as possible. This is still a good place for me to show loving for myself – I take care of my body generally as an act of self-love. I watch what I eat and how much. I exercise regularly and think about my vital organs and what they need for good functioning. I feel good that I can put aside time regularly just for me. I am privileged to have someone listen to me on a regular basis, so that I can reflect on how my life is going and put attention on any hurts that need healing. Life is good, despite all the challenges I face on a daily basis, and I get a real kick from living my life fully.

I believe that my capacity for loving is increasing all the time and it feels like the more love I give, the more I receive. I have a growing circle of friends who do not find it hard to show their appreciation and love of me. I think more of the environment and recycle everything I can. I think of the energy I use, the water I use. I think of the quality time I have with my children and of the state of our relationships. I think more about animals and insects – except for mosquitoes, which really annoy me. I cannot bear their singing any more than I can stand their bite. I have not matched the level of caring of one Rasta friend who just shoos them away – I slap hard; if I was a scientist, they would be number one priority for eradication. Other insects can stay as far as I am concerned; spiders I put outside if they scare my guests. Mice I do not like and recently when I cornered one on my bookshelf he looked me so pitifully in the eye that I just captured him and put him through the front door. When his/her partner appeared a few moments afterwards he/she got the same treatment – my, how things have changed! As boys we used to catch dragonflies, tie thread on them and fly them like kites.

## Expressing love

A masculinity that says men must be tough, strong and often silent is not one that encourages loving expression. Men have been discouraged from showing that they can be caring because this does not fit with the overall socialization for violence. When men internalize the notion that they must be tough, strong and often violent it is contradictory for them to be seen to be caring and loving. As a result most men resent expressions of love in public – how often have you seen men looking embarrassed or awkward with their girlfriend's show of affection on the streets? In some societies men are rarely seen holding their partner's hands; sometimes the woman is allowed to hang on to his arm.

I remember one guy who used to walk hand in hand with his partner – and the whole village knew him too; he stood out for ridicule, from men and also some women. This is the kind of pressure men are under to not show caring. Simply holding hands can single a man out for being "soft" and open to attack. I have at times found myself withdrawing my hands, especially at night, in tough neighbourhoods, fearing it would send the wrong message to potential attackers. For men buying flowers can still invite comment, usually the "what have you done wrong now?" type.

## Relationship-building

Considering the crucial role that relationships play in our lives we have little knowledge and training for sustaining healthy relationships. Couples often do not recognize that when they decide to live together they embark on several relationships: for instance, a financial one, a sexual one, a shopping one, a raising children one, an educational one, etc. It helps to be able to separate the relationships; we often think that because we are good at one the others can be excused. Being a good cook is excellent but it would not compensate for being a terrible lover, and it could soon lead to frustrations in the overall relationship. Looking at the relationships separately gives the opportunity to learn from each other as you work together on the areas that need strengthening. There is a lot you may learn from the way your partner handles finances, and they may learn from you how to cook, for example.

For relationships to work well some fundamental things are crucial:

*Trust:* Without trust our relationships would be consigned to the waste bin. There is no one single element that is more crucial for a relationship. We need to live with some certainty in our lives or we could become extremely stressed. If we had a car that was unreliable to start in the mornings we would soon rid ourselves of it. We need to trust that when we turn the key it will start and we will reach our destination or it is just not worth the trouble. We depend a lot on our relationships to give us some certainty in our existence. We need to trust that our loved ones will behave with a consistency that is expected of them or we will become unsettled. In the same way our lives would be impossible if we could not trust in some very basic things that we pay no attention to or take for granted – for example, that the air we breathe will sustain us, or that the earth we step on would not open up. Without trust or our lives would be unbearable.

Unfortunately many of us find it difficult to trust people as a result of disastrous relationships we encountered when young. Yet we started out trusting; notice how little children who have not been restrained by their care-givers reach out to all around them with the expectation that they will be accepted. It is not until something goes wrong that we lose trust; once we have lost trust it takes a great deal of time and effort to restore it. Nevertheless it is a decision you make and must keep making for your relationship to stand a chance of survival. If you find trusting hard, it is worthwhile examining your past to see where the damage was done so that you can begin to repair it. Your difficulty may have nothing to do with your present partner but with the baggage you carry. This issue cannot be ignored if your relationship is to flourish, and professional help may be necessary to help you restore trust.

**Love:** One only has to listen to love songs to hear the high expectations put on this emotion and its ability to change people and the world. As described by one popular song, it "makes the world go round"- without love our lives would be unbearable. Having a definition of love helps to keep the focus on which behaviours must be changed to fully develop our ability to be lovers. Being abusive and hurtful not only damages your capacity to love but also hinders your partner's ability to love you.

To love unconditionally is something we can all aspire to. There is no greater love; but most of us find it hard to do because of the conditioning we receive in the oppressive society. It is difficult for love and oppression to co-exist. If we truly loved ourselves and other humans there would be none of the mistreatment that the oppressive society depends on for its continuance. We have often had to fight for every bit of our humanity and often our victories have been conditional. It is unsurprising if we love only when love is returned and if we attach all kinds of conditions to loving without being aware of it. For most people, "I love you" usually means *only if you will do or be...whatever*. If you are not ready to give unconditional love, at least be aware of that and spell out what the conditions of your loving are. This way there is less chance for disappointment later on and at least your partner knows what is expected of her/him in the relationship and can choose if they are happy to fulfil those.

**Intimacy:** Being able to share about your life, your fears and dreams with your partners is what helps develop the closeness that is essential in any good relationship. When we keep our dreams and fears from our partners we do not allow intimacy to develop. We all need a safe place to be able to express our dreams and fears, and if we cannot do this in a relationship we need to look at the reasons why this is not possible. Sharing your innermost fears and dreams with your partner makes it more likely that your partner will do the same. Intimacy in a loving relationship can help heal many a past hurtful experience. Of course there are risks involved and I have worked with many couples who have been deeply hurt by partners "throwing in their faces" things that they had shared at the most intimate times. If you are guilty of this type of behaviour you must apologize and be determined that it never happens again or you will no longer be trusted with your partner's innermost thoughts. Sharing every aspect, negative and positive, of our lives is important in developing close relationships

**Honesty:** Honesty is vital to the healthy functioning of any relationship. If we do not believe what is being said, there is no trust; if there is no trust, there is little chance of truly loving. Yet many of us have learned to tell lies. Secrecy and lies serve oppression well as the cornerstone of patriarchal society; it should not surprise that most countries have an official secrets act.

Many of us learn that lying is a necessity if we want to succeed. It takes some learning to be effective liars. But lying often does not sit easily with us, as we give up a bit of ourselves when we tell lies. If you find yourself lying in situations when it was not merited in any way, then you know it has becomes a habit. Being honest in everything we do is liberating, for it removes a great source of dissonance in our lives. Without honesty there can be no trust; without trust there is no love. Men have learned to lie about their true feelings; indeed, that popular soul song of the sixties, "The Great Pretender", would be a fitting epitaph for many. Women, because of the oppression they face, often learn to be deceptive in order to survive. Working at being honest in all things will liberate your relationship.

**Exercise: Breaking the habit.** What is the first lie you ever told and why did you tell it? Take time to think, talk or write about this and make a decision to stop lying.

*Openness:* Most of us have learnt to be secretive about our lives because of the ways we have been hurt early on as young ones. We have had to learn to hide how we truly feel and think or face being hurt even by our closest friends for the way we think. We may be afraid to let our loved ones know where we struggle. Too often we have had hurtful things thrown in our faces in an argument even by those who profess to love us. As a result we have learnt to hide how we really feel and think even from our loved ones. Deciding to be open about your life can be a liberating experience for all.

*Communication:* Many relationships flounder because of a lack of communication. The biggest complaint I hear is of men not listening. We have to learn to do this. Setting aside time for conversation is crucial in maintaining a good relationship. This is why I incorporated taking turns to listen and talk in every group-work session with the men.

If you are able to, make an agreement to listen to each other regularly. It would help to establish a time limit on this exercise and decide to share the time taking turns listening and talking equally. You might start by deciding who talks first. It is good for the person speaking to begin by saying positive things about the person listening before saying the things you would like to see be different. Allowing time to have feelings is good when doing this exercise.

When taking turn at being the one listening you really have to listen and not argue with the things being said; just listen and think about how you can make the changes your partner is asking for. As you listen it is useful to look at your partner with encouragement and admiration. At the end of the agreed time it is your partner's turn to listen to you say positive things about them first, then the things that you want to see changed. You may end the "session time" with a hug.

*Special Time:* Putting aside time just for the two of you. This is crucial for a successful relationship. Doing things that you enjoy together is important; it could be going to the cinema, a meal, a walk or whatever it is you like doing - taking time out to talk, listen to music or watch TV. Just make sure it is time you can have together without others interrupting.

**Relationship building.** When starting a relationship we pay little attention to what can possibly go wrong. It is important to look at some key issues from the outset to give the relationship a real chance of surviving for any length of time. Talking about the things you want and those that you definitely do not want is important. Being open about these things from the beginning gives you both the opportunity to pull back from the relationship if you cannot agree on your differences.

These are some key issues to discuss at the beginning of a relationship:

*Money:* Most people have some distress around money and if there are no clear agreements between partners on how, why and when money will be spent there can be real problems. It is not surprising that the pre-nuptial arrangements favoured by the rich and famous are now spreading to the less affluent. Lack of agreement about how to approach money matters has caused many relationships to flounder. Often perpetrators use money as a means of control; they withhold, remove or take charge of their partner's money.

*Sex:* Nationwide more than four in five women in Britain cited "love, affection and hugs" as what they wanted most from a relationship, with only one in five saying "sex and passion" were most important.[5] This is a topic that is hardly discussed yet it can be quite problematic for relationships. It is important to talk about what you like and dislike sexually and also about frequency, since people have different ideas about what is acceptable. I have often worked with couples who had difficulty agreeing on what was a reasonable frequency of lovemaking; for some it had been either too little or too much.

**Work:** Working lives have an effect on sexual relationships; a recent report showed that some 50 per cent of people who work long hours skip sex when they get home. It was also shown that 35 per cent of people in the UK in full-time work admitted to having had affairs and a further 36 per cent sorely tempted to. Working away from home has obvious problems and changing jobs has led to many a disagreement. Normally the expectation is that the women will follow wherever the man's job leads and this can be problematic for women and children. Sometimes a role reversal is necessary and more and more men are staying at home while the woman "brings in the bacon". This can have a detrimental effect on some men's self-esteem and has to be handled sensitively.

**Children:** There is a lot of pressure put on us to reproduce; someone wants to be an aunt, uncle or a granny. It makes sense to discuss with your partner if you want to have children at all or how many and when. How you would like to raise your children is crucial. There are a great number of good books to help you think about this. It is likely to be the most challenging and rewarding project you will ever embark on, so take time to do your research and come to some understanding on how you would like to approach being parents: or not being parents. The world is already overpopulated and not all of us need be parents.

**Goal setting:** Our lives go better if we have a plan. The final session always ended with this exercise with the men in pairs and taking turns to talk and listen. The person listening making notes for the one talking. Let's take some time to think about the things you want for:

A. Yourself. What is it in life that interests you and what are the things that would truly make you happy? It is good to think about what you need to do to achieve these things; remember, every journey begins with a single step.

B. Your family. Some of you are parents, some may be thinking of becoming parents; those with children obviously need to think about their education, health and happiness. You may have parents, uncles, aunts, siblings or other family members; it is also good to think about these relationships and how you want them to be.

C. Your planet. We have a beautiful planet and we have done much to humanize it. Our lives have never been better, but we now run the risk of completely ruining the planet in a relatively short space of time. It is time to stand back and see what we must change to protect our planet from destruction.

## Closing

The final group-work session with perpetrators is always an emotional event. We have come a long way and much has been said and done. I hope your violence is now something in the past and that you will be able to help other people stop their violence. I know many of you have already started doing this.

We have spent a lot of time learning to take turns at listening and talking – this is a skill for a lifetime and I hope you will continue to practise doing that. We started the group work by looking at the oppression of men. Many will find it hard to accept that men can be oppressed; so you will have your work cut out in being advocates for the liberation of men, but it is absolutely vital that men be liberated from the expectation that we will do violence or we will eventually destroy our beautiful planet. We looked at the role men play in the oppression of women. If we do not interrupt the oppression of women we can never find true happiness. We looked at the way patriarchy has set men up to be the oppressors of women; it has a beginning and must have an ending - it is up to each of us to change this oppressive system.

We had a look at parenting and early socialization for violence. Much of the oppressive patterns of behaviour we learnt are a result of mistreatment and misinformation we received as children. Those that have studied this issue for many years are very clear that "violence breeds violence", so I hope that you will raise your children without the use of violence. We also looked at the way addictions contribute to violent behaviour and have done some work on giving up addictions. For some of you, your relationships have ended but you will go on to have other relationships. This final session I hope will stand you in good stead for having relationships free from violence and based on true love and respect.

I have learnt a lot from you in the process and I wish you every success in your new non-violent life.

# NOTES

## Introduction

[1] British Crime survey 1995.

[2] Amnesty International report, 2001. "Broken bodies, shattered minds: Torture and ill-treatment of women".

[3] Ibid.

[4] Laura Barton, "Sidelines", *Guardian*, 26 May 2005.

[5] Amnesty International report. "Turkish women suffer abuse", in *Guardian*, 3 June 2004.

[6] Musasa Project survey, *The Star* (South Africa), 12 February, 1997.

[7] Amnesty International report 2006.

[8] Catriona Mirrlees-Black, *Domestic Violence: Home Office Research Study 191* (findings from a new British Crime Survey self-completion questionnaire). London: Home Office, 1999.

[9] Amnesty International report, 1999.

[10] bell hooks, *Feminist Theory: from margin to center* (South End Press, 1984).

[11] Survey by Signa, a social research group. *Guardian*, 8 January 2004.

[12] Afua Hirsch, "Domestic violence 'costs £5.8bn' " (quoting Baroness Scotland ahead of her International End Violence to Women Day speech), *Guardian*, 25 November 2008.

[13] Catriona Mirrlees-Black, op. cit. (1999), Domestic violence: Home Office Research Study.

[14] BMA 1998 report.

[15] Justin McCurry, "Japan's domestic abuse cases rise," *Guardian*, 10 March 2006.

16 Purple Berets Fact sheet, "Domestic violence in police families".

17 Andrew Sparrow, "Domestic Violence laws 'backfire'", *Guardian*, 14 April 2008.

18 C. Haney, C. Banks & P. Zimbardo, "Interpersonal dynamics in a simulated prison", *International Journal of Criminology and Penology*, 1 (1973), 69-97.

19 Anonymous, "Degraded for falling in love with a prisoner", *Guardian*, 25 September 2002.

20 Mary Riddell and Jamie Doward, "Madness of dustbin jails - by Lord Chief Justice", *Observer*, 8 October 2006.

21 Eric Allison and Tania Branigan, "Five suicide attempts a day at Holloway", *Guardian*, 9 August 2004.

22 Action for Prisoners Families, press release, 2 March 2005.

23 Eric Allison, "Cherie Booth: keep women out of jail", *Guardian*, 13 May 2004.

24 Roy Walmsley, *World Prison Population List* (8th edition), International Centre for Prison Studies, 2008.

25 Channel 4 documentary, "Short Stories" by Jonathan Barker, 11 December 1992.

26 Dissonance theory. Elliot Aronson, *The Social Animal* (New York: W.H Freeman, 1992), p. 174.

27 Catriona Mirrlees-Black, op. cit. (1999), Home Office Research Study 191 London Home Office.

28 *WHO Multi-Country Study on Women's Health and Domestic Violence against women* (1997). Claudia Garcia-Moreno, Henrica, A. F. M. Jansen, Mary Ellsberg, Lori Heise, Charlotte Watts.

29 bell hooks, *Feminist Theory: From Margin to Center* (South End Press, 1984), p. 130.

# How to Use This Book

1. Gerda Lerner, *The Creation of Patriarchy* (New York/Oxford: OUP, 1986), p. 238.
2. Lerner, op. cit., p. 239.
3. Lerner, op. cit., p. 54.
4. Aronson, op. cit., pp. 174, 175.
5. Aronson, op. cit., p. 35.
6. Harvey Jackins, *The List*, Seattle, WA: Rational Island Publishers, 1997.
7. Aronson, op.cit., p. 285.
8. Catriona Mirrlees-Black, op. cit. (1999), Home Office Research Study 191, London Home Office.
9. Aronson, op. cit., p. 272.

# Chapter One: The Roots of Domestic Violence

1. Lerner, op.cit., p. 89.
2. See, for example, Rhona Ganguly, "Toxic timebomb in city gardens", *Birmingham Mail*, 18 August 2003.
3. Saeed Shah, "Anti-Women cabinet riles Pakistan activists", *Guardian*, 12 October 2008.
4. Lerner, op. cit., p. 36.
5. Lerner, op. cit., p. 135.
6. Lerner, op. cit., p. 136.
7. Ed Harris, "By all means beat your wife, but no more than once a month", *Evening Standard*, 21 August 1996.
8. *Guardian*, 1 April 2002, report from *Gulf News* daily. AP, Dubai.
9. Elliot Aronson, op. cit., p. 36.
10. Murray A. Straus, "Discipline and Deviance: Physical Punishment of Children Violence and other crime in adulthood", *Social Problems*, vol. 38, No 2, May 1991.

# Chapter Two: Men's Liberation

[1] BBC News, 24 May 1999, Mori poll finding, "Men 'need more health care'."

[2] Ibid.

[3] Ibid.

[4] Men's Health Forum website (www.menshealthforum.org.uk).

[5] Office of National Statistics 2002.

[6] Lerner, op. cit., pp. 34, 35, 41. Study by Lawrence Angel.

[7] John Carvel, "Third of men drink to drown out job stress", *Guardian*, 8 June 2006.

[8] Myriam Miedzian, *Boys Will Be Boys: Breaking the Link Between Masculinity and Violence* (New York: Doubleday, 1991), p. 90.

[9] Michael Ellison, "The men can't help it" (review of Palmer and Thornhill, *A Natural History of Rape: Biological Bases of Sexual Coercion*), *Guardian*, 25 January 2000.

[10] Robin Kie and Vanessa Thorpe, "Raging boffins", *Observer*, 22 September 2002.

[11] Aronson, *The Social Animal*, p. 246. Zing Yang Kuo, "Genesis of the cat's love for the rat", *Journal of Comparative Psychology* (Princeton: Van Nostrand), Vol. 11, 1930, p. 24.

[12] Aronson, p. 246. I. Eibel-Eibesfeldt (1963), "Aggressive behaviour and ritualised fighting in animals", in J. H. Masserman (ed.), *Science and Psychoanalysis*, Vol. VI. *Violence and War*. New York: Grune and Stratton.

[13] Aronson, op. cit., p. 246. J. P. Scott (1958). *Aggression*. Chicago: University of Chicago Press.

[14] Aronson, op. cit., p. 247. L. Berkowitz (1968), "The frustration hypothesis revisited", in Leonard Berkowitz (ed.), *Roots of Aggression: A re-examination of the frustration-aggression hypothesis*, New York:

Atherton, 1969.

[15] Ibid.

[16] Aronson, op. cit., p. 247. G. T. Hunt, *The Wars of the Iroquois*. Madison: University of Wisconsin Press, 1940.

[17] Obituaries, Pearce Wright on Ashley Montagu, *Guardian*, 1 December 1999.

[18] Miedzian, op. cit., p. 49.

[19] Lerner, op. cit., p. 17.

[20] Will Woodward, "Girls still choose 'women's jobs'", *Guardian*, 29 November 2001.

[21] Miedzian, op. cit., p.47.

[22] Martin Wainwright, "Man kicked to death outside police station", *Guardian*, 11 December 2006.

[23] History of World War 1. www.historyworld.net.

[24] *Guardian* Editorial, 9 May 2005, "In praise of…immortal memory".

[25] J. K. Galbraith, "A cloud over civilisation", *Guardian*, 15 July 2004.

[26] Aronson, op. cit.: researchers Dane Archer and Rosemary Gartner compared the crime rates of countries at war for roughly 110 countries since 1900; p. 258.

[27] Fox Butterfield, "Wife killings at Fort Reflect Growing Problem in Military", *New York Times*, 29 July 2002.

[28] Mark Townsend, "Minister defends care given to war veterans", *Observer*, 1 March 2009.

[29] BBC News, 20 June 2002, "SAS veteran's suicide plunge".

[30] Chris Mihill, "Celebrations 'reviving war trauma in veterans'", *Guardian*, 27 April 1995.

[31] Mark Gould, "You can teach a man to kill but not to see dying", *Guardian*, 10 October 2007.

[32] PA, "Former soldiers make up 9% of prison population", *Guardian*, News in brief, 1 September 2008.

[33] Oliver Burkeman, "Killed woman in wartime flashback", *Guardian*, 3 March 2001.

[34] Richard Norton-Taylor, "Defence chief welcomes new 'duty of care' deal for forces", *Guardian*, 18 July 2008.

[35] Sarah Ebner, "War's mind field", *Guardian*, 2 May 2001.

[36] Ewen MacAskill, "US question Israel's use of cluster bombs in a rare rebuke", *Guardian*, 30 January 2006.

[37] Richard Norton-Taylor, "US cluster bombs to be banned from UK", *Guardian*, 29 May 2008.

[38] Terry Jones, "Let them eat bombs" Madeline Albright, *Guardian*, 12 April 2005.

[39] Peter Moszynski, "41 countries send children into war", *Guardian*, 13 June 2001.

[40] Polly Curtis, "Mod accused of propaganda in Iraq worksheets for schools", *Guardian*, 14 March 2008.

[41] Human Rights Watch, "International efforts still failing child soldiers", 19 May 2008.

[42] Mark Townsend and Anushka Asthana, "Brown backs army cadet corps plan for schools", *Observer*, 6 April 2008.

[43] "MoD's war on many fronts", *Guardian*, 13 January 2007.

[44] Richard Drayton article, *Guardian*, 10 May 2005.

[45] Helena Smith, "Revealed: the cruel fate of war's rape babies", *Guardian*, 16 April 2000.

[46] Andrew Osborn, "Mass rape ruled a war crime", *Guardian*, 23 February 2001.

[47] City Column edited by Patrick Donovan, "How arms sellers kill off civil exports", *Guardian*, 21 January 1995.

[48] Jason Burke, "Labour pension funds linked to arms traders", *Observer*, 19 March 2002.

[49] The Guardian 21-09-1994 by Geraint Smith "Old soldiers still suffer 50 years on"

[50] Mikhail Gorbachev, "Poison in the air", *Guardian*, 18 June 1999.

[51] Anup Shah, "World Military spending", *Global Issues*, 1 March 2008.

[52] Donald McRae, "Ever sadder reprise of vicious pre-fight threats", *Guardian*, 8 January 1999.

[53] Aronson, op. cit., p. –. D. P. Phillips, "Drop that gun, Captain Video", *Newsweek*, 10 March 1975, pp 81-2.

[54] Janet Sebastian, "Man shot dead over Bruno bout", *Mirror*, 28 April 1992.

[55] Colin Hart, "I don't care if I blind Bruno", *Mirror*, 27 April 1992.

[56] Chris Mihill, "Doctors oppose amateur and professional fights", *Guardian*, 30 November 1991.

[57] Sunday special, "The Lonely Fight", *New York Newsday*, 3 June 1994.

[58] Roy Collins, "Payback time", *Guardian*, 24 January 2000.

[59] BBC News Chanel, 29 December 2008, "Amateur boxing fighting back".

[60] John Carvel, "One in five gay people suffer hate attacks", *Guardian*, 26 June 2008.

[61] News in Brief, "Granddad died to save boy, 11", *Guardian*, 21 February 2000.

[62] Claudia Joseph, "Husband dies trying to save drowning wife", *Today*, 1 April 1995.

[63] Amelia Hill, "Pensioner died trying to save wife", *Observer*, 5 May 2002.

[64] Ian Katz, "Rags to riches man hands out millions", *Guardian*, 23 November 1994.

[65] Sarah Boseley, "Gates gives $750m to fight deadly childhood diseases",

*Guardian*, 25 January 2005.

## Chapter Three: Women's Liberation

1 *International Journal of Women's Studies*, 1983.

2 Amnesty International USA 2006.

3 Quoted in bell hooks, *Ain't I a Woman: Black Women and Feminism* (Pluto Press, 1982), p. 160.

4 Hooper and Tania Branigan, "Pope Warns Feminists", *Guardian*, 31 July 2004.

5 Rory Carroll, "Nicaragua votes to outlaw abortion", *Guardian*, 27 November 2006.

6 John Hiscock, *Telegraph*, 11 June 1998.

7 Lerner, op. cit., p. 29.

8 Lerner, op. cit., p. 235.

9 Diana Elias, "Kuwait's first female minister heckled", *Guardian*, 21 June 2005.

10 Polly Curtis, "Six thousand women missing from boardrooms, politics and courts", *Guardian*, 5 January 2007.

11 Robin McKie, *Observer*, 6 November 2005.

12 Equal Opportunities Commission, 2005, "Then and now: 30 Years of the Sex Discrimination Act".

13 McKie, op. cit., 6 November 2005.

14 Barrie Clement and Patricia Wynn Davies, "Equal pay for women curbed by ministers", *Independent*, 11 October 1993.

15 Lucy Ward, "Firms spurn call for equal pay audits", *Guardian*, 6 March 2009.

16 Julie Finch and Jill Treanor, "Women still tiny minority on UK boards", *Guardian*, 1 August 2003.

17 David Batty, "UK slips further down global gender equality league", *Guardian*, 23 November 2008.

[18] Madeleine Bunting, "It's reigning men", *Guardian*, 29 March 2008.

[19] Jonathan Watts, "China offers parents cash incentives to produce more girls", Guardian, 16 July 2004.

[20] Maggie Michael, "Egypt outlaws circumcision after girl dies", *Guardian*, 1 July 2007.

[21] PA, "Women pay more for cars", *Guardian*, 24 November 2005.

[22] Clancy Chassay, "Acid attacks and rape: growing threat to women who oppose traditional order", *Guardian*, 22 November 2008.

[23] *Feminism Now*. Marcelle d'Argy Smith.

[24] Walter Rodney, *History of the Guyanese Working People*, London: Bogle-L'Ouverture, p. 208.

[25] Aronson, op. cit., p. 311.

[26] Roy Hattersley, "Language and liberty", *Guardian*, 17 April 2006.

[27] Aronson, op. cit., p. 305. Experiments by Ruth Hartley.

[28] *Guardian*. University of Michigan.

[29] Tracy McVeigh, "Girls are now bigger bullies than boys", *Observer*, 10 November 2002.

[30] Lerner, op. cit., p. 218.

[31] Aronson, op. cit., p. 288.

[32] World Health Organization, 2002.

[33] bell hooks, *Feminist Theory:* (South End Press, 1984), p. 81.
Libby Brooks interviews bell hooks, *Guardian*, 26 March 2008.

[34] Lerner, op. cit., pp. 228-9.

[35] bell hooks.

[36]

# Chapter Four: Giving Up Addictions

1 World Drug Report 2006

2 Polly Curtis, *Guardian*, 30 March 2007.

3 World Drug Report 2008.

4 Sarah Boseley on the Gates Foundation, *Guardian*, 24 July 2008.

5 Alexandra Topping, *Guardian*, 30 May 2008.

6 *Use your Brain to Beat Addiction: The complete guide to Understanding and Tackling Addiction*, p. 70.

7 Ibid.

8 Alcohol Concern 2002.

9 National Health Service report entitled *Statics on Alcohol: England 2009*. Sarah Boseley, "One in four adults drinking too much", *Guardian*, 21 May 2009.

10 Ian Sample, "Daily drink may rise cancer risk in women", *Guardian*, 25 February 2009.

11 Amelia Hill, *Observer*, 23 March 2008.

12 Department of Health figures, *Guardian* 18 April 2006, Polly Curtis.

13 Alexandra Topping, *Guardian*, 9 March 2007.

14 James Meikle, *Guardian*, 11 November 2002.

15 *Washington Post*, 9 February 2008, Lori Aratani, White House Office of National Drug Control Policy.

16 Alan Travis, *Guardian*, 26 October 2007.

17 James Randerson, *Guardian*, 7 April 2008.

18 Alok Jha, *Guardian*, 17 April 2008.

19 Poll by Phil Hilton of *Nuts magazine*, Metro, 7 October 2005.

20 Research by Mark Griffiths of Nottingham Trent University. *Guardian*, 10 September 2004.

21 Press Association on Daniel Tuck, *Guardian*, 12 May 2007.

PA, "Rise in gambling addiction is a safe bet, says gambling expert",

[22] *Guardian*, 10 September 2004.

[23] Letter from Professor Peter Collins. University of Salford, *Guardian*, 20 April 2006.

[24] Polly Toynbee, *Guardian*, 18 April 2006.

## Chapter Five: Parenting for Change

[1] Laura Clarke, "Three children killed by abuse in England every week, Baby P probe reveals", *Daily Mail*, 11 December 2008.

[2] 'Dangerous playthings', *Daily Telegraph*, 29 November1994.

[3] John Carvel, "Parents told: you are free to smack", *Guardian*, 8 November 2001.

[4] Martin C. Calder, *Children Living with Domestic Violence: Towards a framework for assessment and intervention*, Russell House Publishing, 2004, p.140.

[5] Stephanie Condron, "Shock new figures on battered women", *Hackney Gazette*, 7 February 2002.

[6] UN Report.

[7] NSPCC study.

[8] *The Observer*, 23 August 2008.

[9] Professor Murray A. Straus, Research paper CP58, 9 June 1998, "New and more definitive evidence about the benefits of avoiding corporal punishment".

[10] UN Report *Violence Against Children*, 2006.

[11] Aronson, op. cit.

[12] Catriona Mirrlees-Black, op. cit. (1999), p. 41.

[13] Aronson, op. cit., p. 258.

[14] Aronson, op. cit., p. 259.

[15] Ibid.

[16] Robert Booth, "Let boys play with toy guns, ministers advise nursery staff", *Guardian*, 29 December 2007.

Aronson, op. cit., p. 260.

[17] Dan Whitcomb, "Calif. Boys charged in 'Sopranos'-style murder",
[18] Reuters, 28 January 2003.

Tim Radford, "Computer games linked to violence", *Guardian*, 24 April
[19] 2000.

Peter McDonald, "US doctors go to war over screen violence", *Guardian*
[20] *International*, 16 June 1995.

Peter McDonald, "US doctors go to war over screen violence".

[21] Kira Cochrane, "For your entertainment", *Guardian*, 1 May 2007.

[22] Rosie Cowan, "UK's 'most violent youth' gets life term", *Guardian*, 17
[23] August 2004.

Paul Webster, *Guardian*, 27 October 1994.

[24] Mike Ellison, "The power and the glory", *Guardian*, 25 October 1994.

[25] David Ward, "Youths charged with murder 'copied Reservoir Dogs'",
[26] *Guardian*, 5 July 2000.

Robert Mendick, Patrick Sawer and Paul Thompson, "Campus gunman's
[27] death video was a direct copy of award-winning Korean revenge movie",
*Evening Standard*, 19 April 2007.

Sheila Lavery, "What makes a great dad?", *Baby World*, October 2007.

[28] Allison Gopnik, "Tears, Tantrums and other experiments", *Guardian*,
[29] 26 January 2000.

## Chapter Six: Building Loving Relationships

[1] Leo Buscaglia, *Love* (Fawcett Crest, 1972), p. 60.

[2] bell hooks, *all about love: new visions* (Women's Press, 2000), p. 6.

[3] hooks, *all about love*, p. 9.

[4] hooks, *all about love*, p. 13.

[5] Findings of the National Sex and Relationship survey, 2002, commissioned by *Top Sante* magazine.

# SELECT BIBLIOGRAPHY

Maya Angelou, *I Know Why the Caged Bird Sings*, 1969.

Elliot Aronson, *The Social Animal*, New York: W. H. Freeman, 1992.

Leonard Berkowitz (ed.), *Roots of Aggression: A re-examination of the frustration-aggression hypothesis*, New York: Atherton Press, 1969.

Leo Buscaglia, *Love*, Fawcett Crest, 1972.

Angela Davis, *Women, Race and Class*, 1981.

Paolo Freire, *The Pedagogy of the Oppressed*, 1972.

Alison Gopnik, Patricia K. Kuhl, Andrew Meltzoff, *How Babies Think: The Science of Childhood*, 1999.

bell hooks, *Ain't I a Woman?: Black Women and Feminism*, London: Pluto Press, 1982.

bell hooks, *All About Love: New Visions*, Women's Press, 2000.

bell hooks, *Feminist Theory – from margin to center*, South End Press, 1984.

Harvey Jackins, *The List*, Seattle, WA: Rational Island Publishers, 1997.

Oliver James, *"They F*** You Up": How to Survive Family Life*, 2007.

Penelope Leach, *Children First: What Society Must Do - And Is Not Doing - For Children Today*, 1994.

Gerda Lerner, *The Creation of Patriarchy*, New York: Oxford University Press, 1986.

Isha McKenzie-Mavinga, *Black Issues in the Therapeutic Process*, Basingstoke: Palgrave Macmillan, 2009.

Myriam Miedzian, *Boys Will Be Boys: Breaking the Link Between Masculinity and Violence*, New York: Doubleday, 1991.

Catriona Mirrlees-Black, *Domestic Violence: Findings from a New British Crime Survey Self-Completion Questionnaire*, Home Office Research Study 191, London: Home Office, 1999.

M. Scott Peck, *The Road Less Travelled: A New Psychology of Love*,

*Traditional Values and Spiritual Growth*, 2003.

Angela Phillips, *The Trouble With Boys: Parenting the men of the future*, London: Pandora, 1993.

Steven Pinker, *The Blank Slate: The Modern Denial of Human Nature*, 2002.

## OTHER RESOURCES

The Everyman Project. A London-based centre that works with and supports male perpetrators of domestic violence. Tel: 020 7263 8884. www.everymanproject.co.uk

Women's Aid. The key national charity working to end domestic violence against women and children.

P.O. Box Bristol 391, BS99 7WS. Tel: 0117 944 4411

Helpline: helpline@womensaid.org.uk http://www.womensaid.org.uk/

# INDEX

**Forthcoming titles from Bogle-L'Ouverture Press:**

*Caribbean Workers Struggles*

By Richard Hart.

Introduction by Kimani Nehusi

*Young Wappy Writers*

Compiled and edited by Grace Akuba